Thousands of people today manage their money more wisely because of the influence of Ron Blue. I know of no one more qualified to counsel people on biblically based principles relative to the sensitive issue of transferring wealth to children.

–Steve Douglass
President, Campus Crusade for Christ

Splitting Heirs is a superb book for anyone needing guidance in wise estate planning—and that includes all of us. Drawing on his years of experience, Ron Blue has authored a book that is practical, wonderfully written, and packed with wisdom. I heartily recommend it.

–Howard Dayton
CEO, Crown Financial Ministries

Time would be well spent to read the "words of wisdom" in Ron Blue's book Splitting Heirs.

–S. Truett Cathy
CEO and Founder, Chick-fil-A, Inc.

This is the first book you'll read that will really prove itself effective when you're gone. But given the choice of "hoping" that all goes well with your children after you die and "knowing," I strongly recommend that you choose "knowing" rather than just "hoping." This is one of the most important books you'll ever read.

–Robert Wolgemuth
Bestselling author of *She Calls Me Daddy*

Splitting Heirs provides readers the opportunity to take advantage of Ron Blue's wealth of experience in financial management. He brings the light of God's Word to bear on an issue that is both practical and crucial for Christians who view the stewardship of resources as a divine trust.

–Andy Stanley
Pastor, North Point Community Church

Thanks to Ron Blue and Jeremy White, a deepened perspective on how we handle our "treasure" is provided. So affluent a cluture as ours easily dulls our discernment, making us—and especially our children—prey to the world-spirit of entitlement and selfishness. In Splitting Heirs our senses are sharpened;

showing us how to plan our will according to the ultimate Will—the Word of God; calling us to wiser stewardship, judicious parenting, and a God-honoring way to handle what we "can't take with us."
–Jack W. Hayford
Pastor, The Church on the Way

Splitting Heirs is interesting and full of facts. More important, it is a book filled with wisdom and understanding. Must reading for thoughtful parents and grandparents.
–Bill Armstrong
Colorado businessman
U.S. Senator 1979–1991

Inheritance is risky business, often damaging lives, marriages, and children. Few of us bring an eternal perspective to leaving money behind or to handling unearned wealth. But God has entrusted us with His assets, and we need to consider how best to invest them in eternity. Ron Blue sets our sights high, offering biblical and practical insights on a vital subject. Ron has written some fine books, but none more important or timely than this one.
–Randy Alcorn
Author of Money, Possessions and Eternity
and The Treasure Principle

One of the most frequestly asked questions at donor meetings is how much do I give to my children and grandchildren? For years Ron Blue has helped donors understand what to do and not do in passing wealth on to the next generation while being a good steward with furthering Christ's Kingdom.
–Hugh O. Maclellan Jr.
President, Maclellan Foundation

As parents and grandparents, Martie and I have wrestled with the questions addressed in Splitting Heirs. How can we best plan for the material resources God has blessed us with in this life? Ron Blue uses the template of God's Word to filter his experience as a financial manager and brings insight to this crucial issue for Christians who want to finish well!
–Joseph M. Stowell
Teaching Pastor, Harvest Bible Chapel

RON BLUE

WITH JEREMY WHITE

Splitting
HEIRS

Giving Your Money and Things to Your Children
Without Ruining Their Lives

NORTHFIELD PUBLISHING
CHICAGO

All Scripture quotations are taken from the *Holy Bible, New International Version*®. NIV®. Copyright © 1973, 1978, 1984 by International Bible Society. Used by permission of Zondervan Publishing House. All rights reserved.

Published in association with the literary agency of Wolgemuth & Associates.

Cover Design: Smart Guys design
Interior Design: Ragont Design
Editor: Cheryl Dunlop

Library of Congress Cataloging-in-Publication Data

Blue, Ron, 1942-
    Splitting heirs : giving your money and things to your children without ruining their lives / by Ron Blue.
        p. cm.
    Includes bibliographical references.
    ISBN-10: 0-8024-1376-5
    ISBN-13: 978-0-8024-1376-5
    1. Estate planning—United States. 2. Finance, Personal—Religious aspects—Christianity. I. Title.
KF750.Z9 B58 2004
332.024'016—dc22

                                                                    2003025234

We hope you enjoy this book from Northfield Publishing. Our goal is to provide high-quality, thought-provoking books and products that connect truth to your real needs and challenges. For more information on other books and products written and produced from a biblical perspective, go to www.moodypublishers.com or write to:

Northfield Publishing
215 West Locust Street
Chicago, IL 60610

3 5 7 9 10 8 6 4

Printed in the United States of America

This book is dedicated to my good friend,
Dr. James Dobson.

Over the past twenty years, I have had the privilege of working with him in many different settings. Dr. Dobson and I have discussed at length the subject of this book and, over time, have come to be in almost total agreement that the wealth that God has blessed us with must, first of all, be used for kingdom purposes. We both feel strongly that there is great potential damage to the second, third, and fourth generation when significant wealth is transferred to them. Jim has challenged my thinking in this area and I deeply appreciate his passion for this important issue. I am honored to call him my friend.

CONTENTS

ACKNOWLEDGMENTS

RON BLUE'S ACKNOWLEDGMENTS

Scripture says, "For you know the grace of our Lord Jesus Christ that, though He was rich, yet for your sakes He became poor that we, through His poverty, might become rich." I want to acknowledge my Lord and Savior as one who understands wealth transfer and its consequences on the recipients better than anyone. It has been my heart's desire that what is contained in this book be honoring to Him and I want to acknowledge that there would be nothing of any value in this book apart from Him and what He has allowed me to experience in my life.

I also want to acknowledge Jeremy White as one who has taken what I have been communicating over the years and put it into a very readable form. He is an incredibly gifted communicator and it has been a privilege to work with him on this book.

I also want to acknowledge Robert Wolgemuth, my agent, and

Greg Thornton and his team at Moody for capturing the vision of the impact that this book might have on kingdom finances. These are more than people that I work with; these are friends and I appreciate them greatly.

Lastly, I want to acknowledge my wife, Judy. Much of what is contained in this book is the result of what I have learned through our thirty-eight years of marriage. She has been a wonderful encourager and partner over those years.

JEREMY WHITE'S ACKNOWLEDGMENTS

Thorton Wilder wrote in *The Matchmaker*, "Money is like manure; it's not worth a thing unless it's spread around encouraging young things to grow." Ron Blue developed the framework for helping people to transfer their manure, er . . . money . . . effectively. What a pleasure for me to help Ron develop that framework into this book.

I am very grateful for the ultimate inheritance that followers of Jesus Christ have through Him. Such lavish grace He provides, but no spoiling.

I would like to thank my outstanding support team of Kris White, Pam Estes, S. L. Highton, and Todd White.

"I love my father, but he's difficult to talk to.
By the way, are you going to bill me
full price for this session, Dad?"

Stu's Views

"Mr. Frosty, it's March.
Time to talk estate planning."

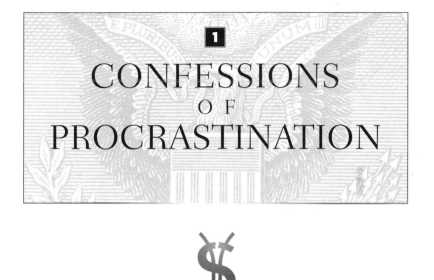

1

CONFESSIONS
OF
PROCRASTINATION

I need to make a confession. Well, maybe two.

Over the years, I had returned to my hometown of Lafayette, Indiana, for reunions and holiday visits to my parents. Like a Norman Rockwell print come to life, Lafayette has a town square at the heart of its business district, a railroad at the heart of its midsection, and a local high school basketball team at the heart of its entertainment.

I had bored my children on previous visits talking about my old stomping grounds. They heard the usual reflective stories, with very little exaggeration, about how I dominated the sports scene at school, how I walked miles to school uphill both ways, and how I often shoveled three feet of snow off the widows' sidewalks on the way for no pay.

But in 1991, I returned to Lafayette for the funeral of my mother. Heart disease ended her life journey from an immigrant's daughter and a faithful spouse of fifty years to a devoted mother of three boys. My mind was flooded with many fond memories of my mom and my childhood. The first important woman in my life was gone.

My two younger brothers and I had never experienced death in our immediate family. Dad was facing the loss of the woman with whom he'd spent a lifetime. He'd gone through so much with her— the ups and downs of life in small town America. The sense of loss weighed mightily. We all knew that a big part of our lives was gone.

But we were men. We could handle this. It's life, part of God's plan. She's in a better place. It would be okay. Time would heal the hurt. You know, I realized clichés are clichés for good reason— though they ring true, they ring hollow. They had no healing power for my heartache or sadness, no relief for my loss.

We four men stood at the funeral, shoulder to shoulder. Emotions suppressed and faces stoic. Sweaty hands folded and clasped behind us. We hardly spoke. It was a beautiful funeral service with tender words sincerely expressed by loved ones and well-wishers. Now it was over.

As we were driving home my wife, Judy, said, "I was wondering how you men would handle this. It fascinated me to see how you four men were so nonemotional and unsentimental." It was an understandable observation. Dad, my brothers David and Wendel, and I were not expressive types. Having emotions is one thing, but expressing them is another. What's a grown, professional man supposed to do at his mother's funeral? Cry? Be a tower of strength? Look solemn and controlled? This was a new experience for all of us.

I know I was sad though. I also know that I never said all the things I would have liked to say while Mom was alive. The day Mom died at the hospital, I happened to be alone in their house before the rest of the family returned. As I was quietly walking through the house, I saw a yellow note on the kitchen table in her handwriting: "Call Ron." A phone call that I wish had happened but didn't.

I wanted to do better with Dad, but that meant man-to-man talk. Son to father. That was not going to be easy. Dad had graduated from high school and worked in a factory; he was a self-made, hard-working man. Well respected in the community, he eventually became mayor of Lafayette. He was a part of that generation that lived with a lot of privacy. I never remember him saying, "I love you." In my forties I finally told him I loved him, and then he told me he loved me. It was a bit like getting an eight-year-old boy to say "sorry" to his little sister—the words didn't come out easily. That was the first time we hugged each other as adults.

Time passed without my bringing up such difficult conversations. Life was moving along like swift rapids. My business in Atlanta was demanding, challenging, and rewarding during the boom years of the 1990s. Our children were growing up, finishing college, and getting married. We were becoming grandparents.

As for my dad? Like any widower or widow, he moped a little and coped a lot. He remarried a couple of years after Mom's death. His new wife, Edna, was a wonderful companion for him. Things seemed back to normal. And "normal" included we men not talking to each other about matters much beyond news, sports, business, and weather.

Several years later, Dad began to have lung trouble. In 2001 I got "the call" to go back to Lafayette because Dad's lung disease had advanced dramatically. He was in the hospital again. We knew he had an incurable, fatal illness, but none of us knew when it would take him. All of a sudden it seemed the moment was upon us. The end-of-game buzzer was about to sound. I realized any discussion of his final plans must start with me.

Driving to the hospital on a drab, gray day, I turned on familiar streets that hadn't changed much in nearly fifty years. Once this was my world, but since leaving home I'd lived in New York, San Francisco, Dallas, and Atlanta. I was privileged to travel to Tokyo, London, Nairobi, Johannesburg, and Hong Kong. Lafayette seemed rather small and ordinary. I was struck by the reality that the world I'd grown up in and the world I now lived in might as well be on different continents. And the same was true for Dad and me. We seemed to be in different worlds.

Dad was in the same community hospital in which I was born. It's curious how birth and death stand side by side. Odd neighbors indeed. I'd been at this unspectacular brick box of a building over the years to visit various friends and relatives, but today was different. It was beckoning me to a final meeting with my dad. What would he say? An even more unnerving thought: What would I say?

I knew I'd not done well with my desire to communicate better with him following Mom's death. My rationalization? If anyone had permission to communicate poorly with his family, as an accountant I did! Being a "numbers guy," I wasn't supposed to be the world's best communicator.

So, here's my confession. My father was eighty-three years old and within forty-eight hours of death. I was headed to his bedside without ever having had a single conversation with him about how to handle things after his death.

I had worked on estate plans for hundreds of clients, written books about family financial matters, spoken to many conferences and charitable organizations about estate planning. But I knew very little of Dad's finances, was unsure what was in his will, and had no idea how he wanted to dispose of assets. During all those visits and phone calls over the years, we'd never talked about what to do upon his death. I knew the biblical principles of finance and wealth transfer yet hadn't talked to Dad about his final affairs.

I pulled up at the hospital and slowly walked inside. It smelled of cleaning solution and didn't look like any interior decorator had ever worked it over. Some nurses bustled by, while others bent over desks cluttered with papers and computers. I found my way along the corridors to his room.

Surprisingly, Dad didn't look like a man who was dying. His mind was in great shape, and he was talkative. But his breathing was labored like a man with a heavy weight on his chest. Dad knew he would never return home, and I did too. This would probably be our last time to talk.

I was relieved when Dad brought up the matter of his last wishes. Most of his desires were pretty straightforward—divide his stuff equally among the three sons. But there was one point where Dad got emotional. He wanted my middle brother, David, to have his car. He had not put this in his will. But with anxiety in his voice, he was urgently telling me, his oldest son, to take care of it.

Many years earlier Dad had helped Wendel and me each get a good car at a crucial point in our lives, but not David. He wanted to make that right. He knew David needed the car more than Wendel or I did. A simple yet loving last gesture from a father who wanted his sons treated fairly.

Dad talked about a few funeral matters and some issues related to the care of his wife. His lucid discussion and heartfelt desire to help my brother were bright spots in a dreary day. We finished, I told him I loved him, and I left. It was my last conversation alone with my father.

I'm sure scenes like I've described occur all over the country every day. Working with thousands of clients over the years, I've seen it regularly. In fact I've seen it at both ends—older folks who haven't prepared their heirs and younger folks who haven't asked if they can be of assistance in any way as their parents prepare for their aging years.

It's common for parents to leave these matters to the last days or last minutes of life. But we don't always know when those last days will be. Judy and I were dating when her father, a promising young doctor, learned he had cancer. After all the years of school and residency and getting his practice established, he and his family were beginning to enjoy the high income of a physician.

Judy and I accelerated our wedding date so her dad could walk her down the aisle. Tragically, he didn't make it. Our wedding was filled with mixed emotions—we had just seen many of our wedding guests a few weeks earlier at a funeral.

Despite my father-in-law's education and sophistication, he hadn't prepared his family for his death. One of his best friends sold life insurance, but he hadn't bought any. Within months of his death, Judy's mom had to return to work as a nurse at age forty-three. Judy's youngest brother, about twelve at the time, had lost not only his father to death, but also his mother to the workforce. Later they sold their house and moved to an apartment. Judy's mom struggled financially for many years because her husband did not prepare properly. It didn't have to be that way.

BEGINNING A BURDEN, IGNITING A PASSION

When Dad died, he was the last of Judy's and my parents to pass away. After his memorial service, I realized that I was kind of the head of the clan now. As oldest son and already a grandfather, I knew I had a position of responsibility in the family. I wanted to do a better job planning and discussing my estate with my children than I had done with my father. We needed to break the silence on matters of death, asset transfer, charitable giving, and preparing our children for what they might or might not receive.

Analysts project that $41 trillion (that's right, this number has a "t" on it) of wealth will transfer in the United States over the next fifty years.[1] A trillion is a million of one millions. Do you know how long it would take to count to a trillion? If you counted nonstop with no bathroom breaks, without eating or sleeping, it would take 31,710 years to count to one trillion. It would be a boring 1.3 million years to count to $41 trillion. As big and unimaginable as the U.S. government debt is, it is only one-sixth of the amount that will move out of the hands of one generation into another.

Dad and I didn't do it right. Judy's dad didn't do it right. I see others doing it wrong every day. I have a burden to see all this change—starting with you. You don't have to make the same mistakes. Some adult children are about to inherit a sum that has the capacity to change their lives—for better or worse. Some charities may—or may not—receive bequests that could help them make lasting spiritual, cultural, or medical changes.

One would think that this issue of wealth transfer involving trillions and trillions would be big news. Surely, people would be talking about this, acting upon it, seizing opportunities, making plans. But seeing the same problem on both sides of my family across forty years and with many others time after time, I find that most people have done nothing.

Oh, they may have a will—but it is often out of date. And they almost certainly have not had those important conversations with children and family members that prepare them for what they will face after parents die. Most of us feel quite unprepared for that type of family discussion. We are intimidated by the emotions it might bring out. That's why I've written this book to help people— rich and not-so-rich, men and women, young and old—success- fully complete a difficult and complex process.

I think there is a better way. And I've found that there are bib- lical principles that can guide us through this process of prepar- ing for "when," not "if," something happens. From a straightforward financial man, here are the straightforward realities:

(1) We will all die.
(2) We will take nothing with us.
(3) We will probably die at a time other than when we would like.
(4) Someone else will get our stuff.
(5) We can decide only *before* we die who gets our stuff *after* we die.

WHY KEEP READING A BOOK REMINDING ME OF DEATH— ESPECIALLY MINE?

Necessarily, this book will discuss death. But it does so in the context of helping you live life to the fullest. In the Bible, Paul tells Timothy of the goal to "take hold of the life that is truly life" (1 Timothy 6:19). I want you to be one of the few, the proud, the ones who finish well. We can still laugh at ourselves in the midst of a serious topic. That's why I have included cartoons at the beginning of each chapter. We might as well smile as we grapple with the challenges of death.

Some estate planning books focus on the challenges of the super-rich and their desire to reduce estate taxes. Such books are usually written on a technical level and focus on complicated trusts, foundations, and techniques. Rather than focus solely on the legal, financial, and technical aspects of estate planning and inheritances, I think readers can benefit from the relational and spiritual dimensions of wealth transfer. So, much of this book deals with family relations (and conflicts), the importance of giving, and God's principles and promises.

News articles and popular culture often focus on high-profile family feuds. Their typical case study is Dad the Entrepreneur and Control Freak who founded a successful company and is worth hundreds of millions.

Dad the Entrepreneur and Control Freak spends a modest fortune on complicated schemes with Good Ol' Boy Lawyer to keep the Old Wife and her New Husband from getting the riches. Or, the so-called estate planning gets messier when there is a remarriage. Dad the Control Freak doesn't want the Old Wife to take all the money away from his New Young Greedy Wife. The Old and Resentful Kids try to influence Dad the Control Freak to exclude the Young Spoiled Kids of New Young Greedy Wife from an equal inheritance. Some of the Old and Resentful Kids have worked for years in the company to get Dad's approval; others have rebellious lifestyles.

On and on such disputes go with negative generational impact on family relations, diminished personal drive and purpose of the children and grandchildren, excessive legal fees, and wasted energy.

For the most part, these situations make tantalizing headlines or entertaining movies. These plots do happen in real life, but they represent a small percentage of families and estates. I intentionally designed this book to apply to middle-class American families as well as the very wealthy. The typical family in America has more wealth than they realize, family relational challenges, and the bedeviling inertia and procrastination toward death matters.

In my research for this book, I did find modern-day examples of well-known individuals doing it right. I have included some of those in the "Just Do It Right!" section at the end of each chapter. I hope they inspire you. However, the principles you will read in this book apply not only to those with estates worth $25 million but also to those worth $25,000.

Why Does This Book Discuss These Financial Challenges?

Looking back over the ten financial books I have written, I realize that they correspond to the life stages my family has gone through. My first book, *Master Your Money,* discussed basic financial planning principles. It dealt with issues we faced while buying houses and cars, avoiding debt, saving for the future, and planning for the unexpected expenses of raising a family.

As we dealt with our five children during the pre-adolescent and teen years, Judy and I wrote *Raising Money-Smart Kids.* In response to concerns in the early 1990s about recessions and a possible economic earthquake, I wrote *Storm Shelter* to help answer what each person should do to prepare for tough economic times.

Toward the end of the prosperous 1990s, I wrote *Generous*

Living to encourage contentment and a giving lifestyle. After entering the latter half of life and an empty nest, I began facing new issues of whether or when to retire, health care and long-term care costs, and investing to last. Larry Burkett and I teamed up to write *Wealth to Last* to help those fifty and over with the more advanced financial issues they face.

I am now in my sixties with a growing extended family. All of our children have married and we now have six grandchildren. We have more wealth than we thought we would ever have. After our wedding, we lived in a trailer—twenty-eight feet long and six feet wide. It was so small you could sit on the toilet, make dinner, and iron clothes without moving. Those were hard times, but we learned a lot. Our children already enjoy a higher standard of living than we had early in our marriage. I would not want to take opportunities of learning away from my kids by giving them "too much."

Dealing with the challenges of handling the wealth entrusted to me by God is what led to wealth transfer being my primary speaking topic recently, and now this book. I found I wasn't alone. As I discussed the outline of this book with other people close to my age, I found they too struggle to decide the balance of assisting yet not spoiling adult children and providing for family yet furthering God's kingdom purposes. They had difficulty dealing with changing roles and expectations of parenting adult children. Judy and I love our kids, but we do have a full life and schedule. Often it seems to us that our kids assume we're sitting at the kitchen table waiting for their telephone call to help them in some way. We do want to help when we can, but fitting it in with our schedules is not easy.

Cut Me a Big Slice of That Humble Pie

Now, about that other confession. A few months ago I was working on the outline for this book. My computer and I were bonding in my basement study as I sat staring at it trying to get my thoughts organized. The ideas had been swirling around my head for quite some time after I'd spoken about wealth transfer at a Generous Giving conference. The participants responded well, and I felt led of the Lord to keep working on the subject. Now I was converting a hodgepodge of ideas into a book.

I paused to reflect on families I'd known—some who had done a good job and some who had done poorly in transferring their wealth. I leaned back in my chair and stared off in deep thought. As I looked more closely at the shelf right in front of me, I saw my will and Judy's will. Both were unsigned!

We had older wills in place, but we'd been working for nearly two years to revise them. A lot had changed since we had done our wills years ago. All our children had finished college, all were married, six grandchildren had come along, and one child was divorced. Our financial situation was dramatically better too. None of this was the case when we wrote our wills earlier.

Judy and I had spent a lot of time with each other discussing how to design our wealth transfer plans. We had prayed about it. And we'd spent a good bit of money with an attorney to cover everything correctly. The wills were finally finished, all typed up with every correction done, ready to sign.

To be honest, they had been there for more than two months! I'd been putting off signing them. Now my eyes were fixed on them as they seemed to yell, "Gotcha!" at me. I knew better, but I'd been busy. You know, it takes very deliberate action to implement the important, but not urgent, actions like signing our wills, getting witnesses, and finding a notary. I didn't have a particularly good excuse, but I just hadn't done it. As I found out, none of us is immune to the procrastination virus.

My aim is to encourage you throughout this book to follow a process involving principles. I am talking about much more than just having a will. Don't worry—this is not another "you need a will, you could die at any time, do it now" lecture!

I'm speaking of *how you decide* what goes in your will and *how you prepare* your heirs for what you put in it. I'm speaking about *deciding very intentionally* what impact you will have as you live and die. Not leaving your stewardship to chance, but planning it carefully. Any good estate attorney can draw up a will; that's a technical matter. My concern is that you bring biblical principles to your decision-making process. In chapter 2 we will look at the overall process for effective wealth transfer.

WHAT IF...

Your doctor said an aggressive cancer would take your life in less than a month. Would you be spending your last days with lawyers and accountants scrambling to make final plans or enjoying the sweet final moments with your family?

WHAT IF...

Your adult children asked your opinion if they should do any planning and will preparation for their families. What would you say? Have you put into place similar plans to what you would have recommended for your children's families?

MAY I ASK A FOLLOW-UP QUESTION?

Q. *Aren't you a little hard on yourself about your lack of discussions with your dad? Whose responsibility is it to share the final plans and details of one's life? Is it really the child's responsibility to bring it up?*

A. It depends. Generally, I would encourage the steward of the assets, let's say the parents, to initiate those conversations. If you continue reading this book, you will see that I will be encouraging you to discuss your wealth transfer plans. I will also be showing you how to accomplish that within your family.

If the parents do not appear to be likely to start such conversations before they are on their deathbed, then I think it may be appropriate for an adult child to initiate the conversation. That's a sign of maturity.

In my case, I don't think that I am being too hard on myself. With me, I knew Dad didn't like to talk about such topics as death and money. Simply because he didn't bring up the topic of his final wishes didn't excuse me with my financial planning background and training. Similar to the instance I shared about saying "I love you" to my father, I decided to go ahead and initiate that conversation because I doubted he would.

These wealth transfer conversations are not easy conversations to have—which is why they don't happen very often. All of us are usually dealing with challenging family dynamics. But someone needs to step up and say, "We are going to do this because it is the best thing to do."

The adult children sometimes fear too much that their parents may perceive them as greedy and eager for a share of the inheritance pie. To prevent that perception, I recommend children speak tactfully and respectfully to their parents. Adult children should never hint at their own needs when bringing up this topic. Possible conversational soundbites may include the following:

➲ "I want to make sure that *your* wishes are taken care of."

➲ "I'm not prying. I'm not interested in the amounts, but what I am interested in is that *your* wishes are expressed and honored after your death."

➲ "If you don't want to talk to us kids now, that's fine. At least talk to your attorney or accountant or someone that you trust."

JUST DO IT RIGHT!

BEING A WISE AND FAITHFUL "STEWART"

Tension as heavy as the June humidity surrounded the Pine-hurst Golf Course in North Carolina. TV viewers moved to the edge of their seats to see if Tiger Woods or Phil Mickelson might catch the leader in the final, pressure-filled holes of the prestigious U.S. Open golf tournament. Payne Stewart showed his cool as he held off the hard-charging challengers to win his second U.S. Open championship on Father's Day in 1999.

At the top of his game and brimming with confidence, Payne Stewart accepted the trophy and surprised the media by saying, "First of all, I have to give thanks to the Lord. If it weren't for the faith that I have in Him, I wouldn't have been able to have the faith that I had in myself on the golf course."

Later he added, "I'm proud of the fact that my faith in God is so much stronger, and I'm so much more at peace with myself than I've ever been in my life."

Payne, however, would not celebrate another Father's Day with his daughter, Chelsea, and son, Aaron. On October 25, 1999, a small plane plummeted to the ground in South Dakota, killing everyone aboard. Among them were golfing great Payne Stewart, age forty-two, and his agent Robert Fraley, age forty-six.

The following days of tributes, replays of championship shots, and memorial services overlooked another strength of Payne Stewart. He had planned wisely for death—not only spiritually, but also financially. Payne had considered and implemented steps to make sure that his wife, Tracey, and their two children were provided for in the event of his death. Although his life was cut short, the educational plans, medical needs, and lifestyle desires of his family were not cut short.

Although not as widely known as Payne, Robert Fraley also

made wise decisions for his surviving wife, Dixie. Having no children, Robert had made formal arrangements with an "accountability" group of trusted men. This group of men acted as advisers for Dixie to help her with major decisions, assist with practical needs, and keep others from taking advantage of her. They met with her soon after Robert's death because he had already chosen them and defined their roles.

In my experience, it is rare for younger or middle-aged people to have their estate and wealth transfer plans completed. Payne Stewart and Robert Fraley did it right, and their survivors benefit daily from their wisdom.

"You're obsessed with money.
You need to think outside of the bucks!"

THE WEALTH TRANSFER PROCESS AND LIFE OVERVIEW

What makes wealth transfer decisions so difficult? They involve a difficult topic—our ultimate demise on this earth. While we eagerly enjoy planning for fun events, such as vacations and parties, we don't enjoy planning for events surrounding death. Because we don't like unpleasant chores, we often procrastinate. Besides dealing with death, wealth transfer decisions also involve family dynamics and seemingly conflicting interests. Let's begin by thinking through a few of these dynamics and possible conflicts.

TRANSITION TO PARENTING ADULT CHILDREN

Parenting five young kids nearly wore us out. Changing diapers, disciplining, playing referee, teaching values, enduring puberty, and acting as chauffeur took a lot of energy and effort. My wife, Judy, and I thought the toughest parenting challenge was when our kids were under our roof demanding our care and attention.

We recently shared a meal with our friends and mentors, noted author and teacher Dr. Howard Hendricks and his wife, Jeanne. They are about twenty years older than we are and have four kids. Judy and I had recently been dealing with some difficult situations with our adult children. So we asked the Hendricks, "Does parenting adult children soon get easier?"

To our surprise, they said, "No, it gets harder."

But the more we thought about it, the more their statement made sense. The challenges and problems our adult children face are more significant than when they were younger, yet we have less control over them. No longer are we dealing with whether the kids buy designer shoes or not, who can sleep over, whether Johnny can go to camp this summer, or which prom dress Mary wants. Our adult children deal with life issues such as selecting a mate, choosing a career, buying a home, or going through sickness, death, or possible divorce.

Life as a parent may seem backward at times. Just when your children's issues become more significant, you have less control and influence, but more money to give them. So what do you do? It's probably better to avoid "fixing" things for adult children by "buying" solutions. It's so tempting for parents with more wealth than their adult children to throw money at the problems life brings, but doing so can do more harm than good.

Howie and Jeanne have experienced both a divorce and a death among their children. Judy and I didn't anticipate a divorce among our children, but it happened. We hurt for our kids and ourselves as parents, but there is little we can do to control or prevent these life issues. We as parents can encourage, support, pray, and offer some assistance along the way, but grown children, particularly married children, need to be running their own lives.

I will share more in detail about family dynamics in later chapters. You can likely already see a trade-off coming: If I give too much now, it may negatively affect them. Then, how about leaving it all to them at my death?

WHO WILL REALLY END UP WITH MY WEALTH?

If you leave your entire estate to your children, that wealth will likely have more impact on the second and third generations. With the trend of increased longevity, your children will likely be in their fifties or sixties when you and your spouse die. By then, they will have established their lifestyles and habits. I'm sixty-two and Judy is sixty; we are both in good health. Based on current mortality tables, there is a good chance one of us will reach age ninety. Our oldest daughter would be about sixty-five then.

When speaking at conferences, I have regularly asked audiences this question, "Can you tell me the maiden name of one of your great-grandmothers?" Usually no one raises a hand. I'm sure you don't use the maiden name of your maternal great-grandmother as a password on the Internet or as a security question!

My great-grandchildren will probably not know me or be able to remember much about me. If I pass wealth on to them, then it is essentially like passing wealth on to a stranger. I will have had little impact on them. They have no real knowledge of who I am or my value system.

A wealthy friend once asked me if I had ever seen significant wealth successfully transferred to the third or fourth generation. I thought about it for a while and could only think of one family as a possible good example. After I mentioned the family's name, he said, "I know that family better than you do, and you're wrong. The money screwed them all up!"

I used this story as an illustration at a recent conference. Later at the airport a lady who had attended the conference pulled me aside. She told me about her father, who had started a multinational company that is now a household name. She said, "You are right about the potential to change an heir's life negatively. My father's estate had twenty-two heirs to his vast wealth, and only four of them turned out to have a meaningful, productive lifestyle."

In chapter 5, we will discuss some practical ways to help but not harm your children and grandchildren by giving to them. What about simply giving it all away? Then, you certainly wouldn't risk spoiling children or grandchildren! Another challenge . . .

WHICH NEEDS IN GOD'S KINGDOM DO I SUPPORT?

Of the world's 6.4 billion people, only 292 million live in the United States.[1] That's only 4.5 percent. Yet the United States owns or controls over half of the world's wealth. Think of it. Four and one-half percent of the people own most of the assets, most of the world's military technology, and most of the political power.

To break this down a bit further, it has been estimated that of all worldwide wealth controlled by Christians, about 80 percent is controlled by American Christians.

My friend, the late financial author and teacher Larry Burkett, said, "I believe that God has blessed Americans so that they could fund the fulfillment of the Great Commission." I agree with him. From our Christian founding, God has entrusted stewardship of much of the world's resources to America to accomplish His purposes for this period of history. My own belief is that we have a window of opportunity in the United States now that may not be available twenty or thirty years from now.

So, let's take advantage of a time such as this. It may seem overwhelming when you consider all of the needs cleverly marketing themselves through your mailbox, telephone, Internet, or radio, but I believe it is our responsibility to research and choose charities, mission organizations, or specific individuals to support with the wealth God has given us. This responsibility is part of my desire to finish life strong.

Whether held by a country or an individual, it seems more wealth creates more opportunities for failure. Wouldn't it be great to be able to agree with Paul's reflection on his life, "I have fought the good fight, I have finished the race, I have kept the faith" (2 Timothy 4:7).

Of the 2,930 people mentioned in the Bible, Dr. Howard Hendricks observed that you could study and know more detail about the lives of one hundred people. Of those one hundred, where you can trace how they finished their lives on earth, only one-third finished well. Think of the early successes but later failures of Samson, King Saul, Solomon, and Judas. Strong finishers include Job, Elijah, Daniel, Peter, and John.

My observation is that the proportion of Christians finishing well diminishes with the increase of worldly wealth. That's not a criticism of worldly possessions, but an observation of how people tend to treasure their treasure.

WHY IS WEALTH TRANSFER SO CHALLENGING?

Weighing these issues is what makes wealth transfer so challenging. We have briefly touched on some of these issues so far in this chapter. Let me summarize the challenges of planning the transfer of your wealth on the following list:

- Helping your children and grandchildren but not harming them
- Managing expectations of children and spouse
- Dealing with sons-in-law, daughters-in-law, stepchildren, step-grandchildren
- Providing for your spouse
- Providing for God's kingdom purposes
- Deciding what charities or ministries to support
- Avoiding family conflict and sibling jealousy

●Dealing with the reality of your death

●Acknowledging that all of your hard-earned wealth will be left to someone else

●Talking about a difficult subject

●Obtaining agreement with your spouse

●Desiring to control your prized assets or business beyond the grave

●Handling change in personal and family circumstances

●Experiencing significant changes in wealth

●Desiring to finish strong

●Learning about complex legal and financial matters, such as wills, trusts, estate taxes, etc.

Whew! No wonder people (including myself) tend to procrastinate. We all gravitate toward the easy and routine actions rather than the difficult and important ones.

For challenges like these, we need wisdom. The Bible says,

Wisdom, like an inheritance, is a good thing
and benefits those who see the sun.
Wisdom is a shelter
as money is a shelter,
but the advantage of knowledge is this:
that wisdom preserves the life of its possessor.
(Ecclesiastes 7:11–12)

Because wisdom is knowledge applied to life, I want to share my outline of the Wealth Transfer Decision-Making Process. This outline is an application aid. Throughout the rest of the book, we will explore the importance and implication of each decision. Rather than wait until the end of the book, let's get to the punch line right now:

WEALTH TRANSFER
DECISION-MAKING PROCESS

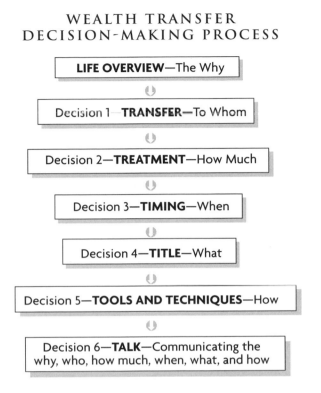

Please note that I have described this chart as a "process." A process should be followed in sequence. Do step 1 before step 2. Never do step 4 until you've done step 3. If you were to try to make a lemon meringue pie and you threw all the ingredients together, you would have a mess. Even though you used the right ingredients in the right amounts, you would not have a good lemon meringue pie unless you followed the steps in sequence.

When attempting estate planning, most people and most professional advisers begin with Decision 5—The Tools and Techniques Decision. This decision includes the technical aspects of drafting a will, avoiding estate taxes, or establishing a trust. But you should first decide who is getting how much. How much do you give to missions and how much to your children? When should you give to either of them—now or at your death? Follow the suggested process for the best outcome.

You may have noticed by now my use of the term "wealth transfer" instead of the term "estate planning." My approach is not the norm in most popular media forms, so the use of "wealth transfer" is very intentional. Its aim is much different than estate planning.

The Approach of Wealth Transfer Is To . . .	The Approach of Estate Planning Is To . . .
Consider impact on recipients as highest priority	Consider impact on the donor and estate
Implement plans that can (and should) begin now	Implement plans that begin at death
Involve family input now and professional advisers later	Involve professional advisers now and family later
Make stewardship decisions	Make tax-efficient decisions
Bring honor to God	Bring honor to oneself
Transfer ownership	Retain control as long as possible—even beyond the grave

HOW MUCH WEALTH DO I HAVE TO TRANSFER?

A businessman wanting to get to the point might ask, "What kind of money are we talking about here?" First, it is helpful for you to have an idea about how much potential wealth you may transfer.

Don't be thrown off by the word *wealth* in wealth transfer. You may think this doesn't apply to you because you are not wealthy. But all of us have to deal with the question: What happens to all my stuff? If you have lived in America, then you are wealthy to the rest of the world.

My experience is that people often have more wealth than they think. The problem is not a lack of wealth, rather that very few people have given much thought to how to use and save assets now, and even less thought to adding it up and dividing it out for after death. As we begin, I recommend you take a moment to use the Quantifying Your Wealth to Transfer worksheet on the following page to see how much wealth you may have available.

Simply input the approximate value of your various assets. Then, add the "unrealized wealth" that may be available later, such as the amount of life insurance to be paid upon your death or future inheritances. Let's say that you are an only child. Your ailing mother's will has named you as receiving her house and CDs totaling $250,000. Although you don't know when your mother will die and you don't count that as your money yet, add it to your estimated wealth to transfer to help you see how much may be within your control someday.

QUANTIFYING YOUR WEALTH TO TRANSFER

Wealth—Available Now:

Cash on hand and checking account $_____

Money market funds   _____

CDs   _____

Savings accounts   _____

401(k) and other retirement plans from your company   _____

IRAs   _____

Pension & profit sharing   _____

Mutual funds   _____

Bonds   _____

Equity in your home   _____
             (market value less remaining mortgage balance)

Land (market value)   _____

Business valuation (market value)   _____

Rental property   _____

Real estate—farm, lots, etc   _____

Limited partnerships   _____

Boat, camper, tractor, etc.   _____

Automobiles   _____

Furniture and personal property (estimated market value) _____

Coin and stamp collections, antiques   _____

Receivables from others   _____

Other:_____   _____

Other:_____   _____

         (A) Total Wealth Available Now $_____

         (B) Appreciation Factor   _____
                 (obtain from the table on next page to estimate
                       your future potential increase of wealth)

         (C) = (A) x (B) Total Estimated Wealth Available $_____

Unrealized Wealth—Available at or After Death

Life insurance proceeds upon your death   _____
Estimated inheritances you may receive later   _____

    (D) Total of Unrealized Wealth $ _____

    (E) = (A) + (D) Total Wealth if Death Occurred Soon $ _____

    (F) = (C) + (D) Total Estimated Wealth Available $ _____
              at Future Date

Appreciation Factor Table:

Estimate the rate of return that your wealth will appreciate each year. Then, estimate the number of years of your life expectancy. Trace over in the table below to the number, or factor, where the two intersect. Use that number above for Item B in the Quantifying Your Wealth to Transfer worksheet.

Estimated Years Until Death	Assumed Annual Rates of Return				
	4%	6%	8%	10%	12%
2	1.08	1.12	1.16	1.21	1.25
5	1.22	1.34	1.47	1.61	1.76
10	1.48	1.79	2.15	2.59	3.10
15	1.80	2.40	3.17	4.18	5.47
20	2.19	3.20	4.66	6.72	9.64
25	2.67	4.29	6.85	10.83	17.00
30	3.24	5.74	10.06	17.44	29.95

Let's work through an example of completing this worksheet. George and Martha are typical of many Americans. Their parents lived through the Depression, worked hard, and did well financially despite not attending college. George and Martha were born just a few years before the baby boomers. They met in college, married, and did better than their parents in terms of education and career. George was a middle manager of a large manufacturing company for thirty years; Martha taught school for twenty years in total after taking a break in service to raise their children.

Now in their late sixties, George and Martha still consider themselves "middle-class"—they enjoy about the same standard of living as their neighbors in their tree-lined, mature neighborhood in the suburbs. As they began to work through their wealth transfer plans, they wrote down the following summary of their assets using the worksheet shown on pages 42–43.

GEORGE & MARTHA—
QUANTIFYING THEIR WEALTH TO TRANSFER

	Wealth—Available Now:
Cash on hand and checking account	$ 10,000
Money market funds	-0-
CDs	50,000
Savings accounts	-0-
401(k) from George's employer	375,000
Roth IRAs	35,000
Martha's teacher deferred compensation plan	60,000
Stock in GM inherited from Martha's father	50,000
U.S. savings bonds	5,000
Home (market value, not original cost)	250,000
Land (market value)	-0-
Business valuation (market value)	-0-
Rental property	-0-
Real estate—undeveloped lot at the lake	75,000
	for possible future home
Limited partnerships	-0-
Boat, camper, tractor, etc.	15,000
Family car and George's truck	30,000
Furniture and personal property (estimated market value)	40,000
Coin and stamp collections, antiques	-0-
Receivables from others—Loan to George's brother	30,000
Other:_____	-0-
Other:_____	-0-
(A) Total Wealth Available Now	$1,025,000

George and Martha could hardly believe that their assets added up to over $1 million. Based on their ages and good health, they believed they could live another twenty years. With a portfolio mix of stock and bond mutual funds in George's 401(k), the real estate appreciation in their area, and CD rates, George thought a 6 percent rate of return was reasonable for their assets. By referring to the Appreciation Factor Table, George selected the factor of 3.2 (20 years at 6%). Assuming that their pensions and Social Security keep paying their monthly bills, George and Martha estimate that their wealth available may total over $3 million in twenty years:

(A) Total of Wealth Available Now	$1,025,000
(B) Appreciation Factor	3.2
(C) = (A) x (B) Total Estimated Wealth Available	$3,280,000

In addition to this, George already knows that his ailing mother will be leaving him a house and a CD totaling $150,000 upon her death. Taking this into account with the life insurance on George and Martha, the following wealth will be available later:

Unrealized Wealth—Not subject to significant appreciation

Life insurance proceeds upon your death	300,000
Estimated inheritances you may receive later	150,000
(D) Total of Unrealized Wealth	$ 450,000
(E) = (A) + (D) Total Wealth if Death Occurred Soon	$1,475,000
(F) = (C) + (D) Total Estimated Wealth Available at Future Date	$ 3,730,000

In my experience, most people are surprised at how much their future estates may be worth. With home values appreciating over a period of years, life insurance, and increased 401(k) and IRA balances, you (or your parents) may be a millionaire after all. Even if you have less than that, you still have much more than most people in the world. Shouldn't you at least consider what is going to happen to those assets and whom they might affect?

PRINCIPLES BEHIND THE PROCESS

During my years of helping others with financial planning and handling our family's financial planning, I have found best decisions are made when they are based on sound principles. Principles last and persevere. Daily stock market changes, inflation estimates, and gold price predictions are just noise. The talking heads on the daily financial news shows make noise we should block out. We shouldn't base important decisions by wetting our fingers, sticking them up in the wind, and guessing which way interest rates will go next month or next year.

For each decision in the Wealth Transfer Decision-Making Process, rely upon one or more biblical principles to guide your thoughts. Please refer to the expanded chart below and on the following page updated with the underlying principles. We will discuss each decision and the related decisions in the following chapters.

WEALTH TRANSFER DECISION-MAKING PROCESS

LIFE OVERVIEW—The Why

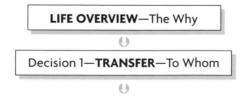

Decision 1—**TRANSFER**—To Whom

THE TREASURE PRINCIPLE ➲ You can't take it with you, but you can send it on ahead.

THE UNITY PRINCIPLE ⮕ Your spouse completes you, not competes with you.

THE WISDOM PRINCIPLE ⮕ Transfer wisdom before wealth.

Decision 2—**TREATMENT**— How Much

THE UNIQUENESS PRINCIPLE ⮕ Love your children equally and treat them uniquely.

Decision 3—**TIMING**— When

THE KINGDOM PRINCIPLE ⮕ Time your wealth transfer to maximize its use by you, your heirs, and kingdom servants.

THE GIVIN' WHILE LIVIN' PRINCIPLE ⮕ Do your givin' while you're livin' so you're knowin' where it's goin'.

Decision 4—**TITLE**— What

THE STEWARDSHIP PRINCIPLE ⮕ God owns it all.

Decision 5—**TOOLS AND TECHNIQUES**— How

THE TOOLS PRINCIPLE ⮕ Estate planning tools and techniques help you accomplish objectives, but are not the objective.

THE TRUST PRINCIPLE ⮕ Never use a trust because of a lack of trust.

THE K.I.S.S. PRINCIPLE ⮕ Keep it as simple as possible.

Decision 6—**TALK**— Communicating the why, who, how much, when, what, and how

THE EXPECTATION PRINCIPLE ⮕ Communicate to align expectations with plans.

LIFE OVERVIEW

Before focusing on each decision, let's step back and look at the big picture. One of the most useful exercises you can do is write out a mission statement for your life. Write down your life purposes.

A key to financial freedom and to effective wealth transfer is understanding our life purposes. God has a general purpose for all believers, such as bringing glory to Him and sharing the good news of God's salvation through Jesus Christ.

Each believer also has specific purposes for life unique to his gifts, talents, contacts, and opportunities. As we prayerfully discern where our gifts and experiences lie, God begins to reveal to us where to spend our efforts, time, emotional energy, and money on those areas. Then, of course, do we obey what He has revealed to us?

Our role as stewards involves both general purposes for our lives—faithfully managing what God has entrusted us with—and specific purposes. God owns it all. All the resources and abilities are within my control only temporarily. As the Bible says,

> And [Job] said, "Naked I came from my mother's womb, and naked I will depart. The LORD gave and the LORD has taken away; may the name of the LORD be praised." In all this, Job did not sin by charging God with wrongdoing. (Job 1:21–22)

This is one rule with no exceptions. Your hearse will not be pulling a U-Haul. Someone asked John D. Rockefeller's accountant if he knew exactly how much Mr. Rockefeller had left when he died. The accountant replied, "Certainly, to the penny. He left everything."

As you live this one life where you take nothing with you, you are writing a story. You are a playwright putting the finishing touches on the story of your life. You get a lot of input on the twists and turns of the plot. You can write a story about how you live with your money and how you leave it. What will the story say? How will that story impact others?

I recently met with a couple with significant wealth. He was a businessman who had sold his successful company for millions of dollars.

His wife of forty-one years made the comment while we were sitting there discussing the sale of his business, "Finally I can replace the dresser in my bedroom." Sensing this sounded interesting, I said, "Tell me what you mean."

She told how they had bought a dresser when they got married. About fifteen years ago, a drawer broke, and they had never repaired it or replaced it. During that time, every day she had been looking at this dresser in their bedroom with a broken empty drawer. This couple earned a very high income for many years. As I glanced at the husband, I sensed he was mentally patting himself on the back for not having bought a new dresser—for saving that money.

I thought to myself, *How could I talk to this guy without offending him?* I first asked him whether he loved his wife. He said he did. That didn't offend him.

Then I continued, "What if that dresser represented to your wife something more than a place to store clothes? For example, the dresser potentially is a statement of who she is because it is a part of what she is allowed to decorate and to manage. Just as you have built a business, she has built a house. She builds the things that are in the house."

As he was processing this, I changed my tone and asked offhandedly, "How much money would you pay for your wife's peace of mind, contentment, and happiness?"

He said, "Well, I'd spend anything."

"Then buy a dresser. My point is that money is a tool. You should spend money to accomplish an objective. Buying something for your wife's peace, such as a new dresser, may be just as important as investing it or giving it away. God gave money to us as a tool to use."

Biblical stewardship is the accomplishment of God-given objectives using God-given resources. I am accountable for all of His resources, not just 10 percent of them. It isn't necessarily more spiritual to give to your church than to spend money on a much-needed family vacation. It's all God's anyway, whether I buy groceries, buy sneakers, or give to the poor.

Now, I can just imagine many wives marking this dresser illustration with a highlighter and showing their husbands, "See what Ron says you should do about that new _____ I have been wanting!"

Don't take me out of context and use this story to justify spending when you haven't planned for it or to justify anger toward a spouse who can't afford to buy you everything you want when you want it. All I am saying is that your financial decisions should relate to using God's resources to accomplish His purposes whether they be buying Bibles to place around the world or buying a dresser for your wife to show her that you desire to bless her.

God's purposes are not money or things. Money and things may represent opportunities to accomplish His goals and objectives while we're here. My point in including this illustration is that the businessman is writing a story. It is one of a wise, frugal, business genius. But it is also a rich man so tight that a gallon of WD-40 couldn't loosen his wallet to spend eight hundred dollars for a dresser. What I urged him to do is include a romance chapter in his life story about his love for his wife.

What story are you writing with your life? Do you have a heart for international missions, prison ministry, or homes for low-income people? Then put your money where your heart is. Better yet, put your plans where your heart is.

WHAT IF...

Your closest friends, your prayer partners, and your pastor read your will. Would they say that your final wishes matched your life mission and purposes?

MAY I ASK A FOLLOW-UP QUESTION?

Q. *Will all Christians reach the same or similar conclusions by using the wealth transfer process you presented?*

A. No. Your spiritual gifts and interests, your family situation, or the nature of your resources may lead you to transfer your wealth very differently from Christian friends. I have tried to present a process of thinking to help you to prayerfully and uniquely conclude what God would have *you* do rather than say a specific, blanket "This is how you should transfer your wealth" to all members of God's family.

Q. *How often should I review my will and estate plans?*

A. I would recommend at least every three years. Perhaps sooner—if you or your family have experienced significant changes.

If you have made a will or set up other wealth transfer techniques, I commend you. Many people never get around to doing that. But then, keep in mind that your wealth transfer plans represent a process. It's really an ongoing process. I have presented in this chapter a framework for you to think through the ongoing wealth transfer process. Don't simply make a will and let it gather dust for thirty years.

As circumstances change, as the world changes, as ministry opportunities change, as tax laws change, and as you learn new information (such as ideas you are reading in this book), you will need to review your plans. Generally, though, I think that reviewing your wealth transfer plans every few years with an adviser is appropriate.

JUST DO IT RIGHT!

A STEELY
DETERMINATION TO GIVE

After working at his first job at age thirteen as a bobbin boy in a cotton mill for $1.20 a week, Andrew Carnegie would spend Saturday afternoons reading from the library of Colonel James Anderson. Carnegie could not afford the subscription fee to borrow books from the so-called "public library." So, he pursued his self-education from Colonel Anderson, who allowed working boys and girls in the Pittsburgh area to read from his books.

Carnegie rose from bobbin boy to a telegraph clerk and later founded his own company, Carnegie Steel Company. He essentially started the steel industry in Pittsburgh and grew his company by supplying the rapidly growing railroad industry with iron and steel. Carnegie became one of the most successful and wealthiest businessmen in America in the late 1800s and early 1900s.

Although considered by some as ruthless in business practices, Carnegie began early in his business career to practice charitable giving. He once said, "The man who dies thus rich dies disgraced."[2] Remembering his childhood experience, Carnegie used much of his fortune for his lifelong interest of building public libraries. When he began to promote his idea, there were few public libraries. Carnegie donated more than $56 million for the building of 2,509 public libraries in the English-speaking world.

Carnegie was perhaps the first of the very wealthy to advocate publicly that the rich had a moral obligation to give away their fortunes.[3] Credited as a father of scientific philanthropy, Carnegie strongly urged that a thoughtful consideration and process be given to dividing wealth. He sought to apply business and management principles to administer his wealth transfer.

In several published essays, he laid out his "Gospel of Wealth." His main arguments were the following:

(1) Do not leave large sums of money to heirs and possibly spoil them.
(2) The estate tax is the wisest form of taxation by society to discourage the hoarding of millionaires and to encourage better use by the community.
(3) This taxation should induce the rich man to administer his wealth during his life while he possesses the knowledge to give it away most wisely.

In a letter to himself, he committed to stop working in two more years and pursue a life of more education, giving away his fortune, and benefiting others. He wrote, "Man must have an idol—the amassing of wealth is one of the worst species of idolatry—no idol more debasing than the worship of money."

In the latter part of his career, he did devote his full-time efforts to giving away his fortune. Much to his dismay, he found his other investments kept increasing and that he had trouble giving it away fast enough. He began giving to fund private universities (Carnegie Mellon University), the arts (Carnegie Hall), pensions for schoolteachers (now known as TIAA-CREF), and peace projects. It is estimated he gave away 90 percent of his wealth during his lifetime.[4]

Carnegie's concluding paragraph of the Gospel of Wealth indicates he understood his role of stewardship:

This, then is held to be the duty of the man of Wealth: First, to set an example of modest, unostentatious living, shunning display or extravagance; to provide moderately for the legitimate wants of those dependent upon him; and after doing so to consider all surplus revenues which come to him simply as trust funds, which he is called upon to administer.[5]

Stu's Views

"No, you can't get an advance
on your inheritance."

YOUR
TRANSFER
DECISION

The dedication of this book to my friend Dr. James Dobson, family psychologist and founder of Focus on the Family, didn't happen in the usual way of the book-publishing world.

Jim has often invited me to speak to small groups of significant donors to Focus on the Family at a ranch in Elk Canyon, Montana. I usually speak about the principles of training children to manage money. Because the participants usually have significant wealth, I would also discuss wealth transfer to adult children and how to do it.

Invariably, Jim gets up after me and says, "I agree with almost everything Ron has ever written and spoken about, except in this area. I don't think anything good can happen if you transfer wealth to children." It became an unscheduled routine in the program that we would have a friendly debate about this issue.

Jim's personal perspective, having grown up in a pastor's home with very little financial wealth, was that money does more harm than good for children's motivation, faith, and ability to learn life's lessons. He had also seen in his professional counseling experiences that significant inheritances have significant negative consequences in the lives of children inheriting the money.

I would respond with Proverbs 13:22, "A good man leaves an inheritance for his children's children." Although I didn't say people were forced to leave it to their kids, I did say that doing so was fine if parents had taught their kids wisely. The small group of participants in the informal retreat setting usually seemed to enjoy our banter.

Recently, I was a guest panelist on Focus on the Family's radio program discussing the topic "Caring for Aging Parents." The panelists of doctors and family counselors discussed the various medical and emotional issues of adult children and their aging parents. Then, the conversation turned to the financial issues. Jim said, "Ron, now I am going to ask you a question, and this is the only area where we have disagreement."

I gave a broad smile, and he said on the air, "You know what I am going to ask you, don't you?"

"Yes, I do," I replied knowingly.

He said, "What do you think about transferring money and possessions to adult children?"

"Jim, as I've gotten older, I have come closer to your way of thinking on this. I can see very little good happening to the children or to the family's stewardship by transferring wealth to adult children." I told him about this book that would help readers figure out wise choices for the inheritance of their assets.

Although he has nearly thirty years of radio experience, he seemed surprised. He laughed and remarked, "Well, I hope you are going to dedicate the book to me!"

I replied offhandedly, forgetting the Focus on the Family broadcast is heard by millions around the world, "OK, I will . . . if you will write the foreword!" The other panelists—while we were on the air—urged Jim to do that.

After the radio program was over, I met with Jim privately in his office. "Jim, I know your board of directors has a policy of you not writing forewords to books. My comment was a spontaneous one. I didn't mean to put you on the spot. I really am planning to write a book about the wealth transfer process. You don't have to write the foreword."

He said that he would like to read the book when I was done and would endorse it. He felt strongly that such a book urging a deliberative process was needed rather than the usual default of leaving everything to adult children.

So, let's begin thinking deliberately about the risks and rewards of transferring wealth to heirs—whether those heirs are ministries or your family.

THE GOOD STEWARD'S FINAL PRIVILEGE

God owns it all. My name may be attached to all the accounts and property under my control, but my name is on them only temporarily. I'm only a steward, and I'm going to leave it all behind. But I'm able to choose His next steward.

The process of wealth transfer is essentially a spiritual exercise. It is not merely a financial or legal matter. We have to work it out in the presence of God and to His glory. What a marvelous privilege God has granted us to select His next stewards. But with such privilege comes great responsibility. As Jesus said, "From everyone who has been given much, much will be demanded; and from the one who has been entrusted with much, much more will be asked" (Luke 12:48b).

If we place His stuff in the hands of unworthy stewards, I suspect God will find a way to take it away from them. Still, part of being a good steward includes choosing and preparing the next best steward. What are your options of choosing stewards? Looking at the big picture, you have only three choices for the next steward:

1. Your heirs
2. Charity
3. Government (by taxes)

Your heirs. These are individuals you choose, usually your family. Whether by default or design, this is the most popular choice of Americans. From a tax and estate planning view, this is a poor choice because estate taxes often eat up a significant chunk of the wealth. If your estate is large enough to pay estate tax, then let me give you a rough estimate of your taxes. For every dollar you leave to your heirs, you will leave an extra 85 cents for the government. So, it will take $1.85 of assets to leave a dollar! Sounds drastic, this death tax. That's just the way the estate tax rates work. According to the amount of your estate, the estate tax rates rise to nearly 50 percent. If you want to leave $3 million to your kids, you will need a lot more than $3 million to do it. (By the way, you can reduce or eliminate your estate taxes with proper planning. We'll talk in more detail about taxes in chapter 7.)

The common strategy with most people, including Christians, is to keep as much as possible while they're alive, then leave it all to their heirs upon their death. Unfortunately, the heirs are usually poorly trained to manage the assets. Wouldn't it be a shame for your wealth to ruin your children or grandchildren?

Numerous support groups, Websites, and self-help books are devoted to helping inheritors of wealth cope with their problems. Because we cling to the mistaken notion that a few million dollars will solve anyone's problems, we scoff at the notion of the wealthy having difficulties. We don't anticipate the lack of self-esteem, the guilt for having so much, or the difficulty in developing deep relationships because of too much suspicion or lack of trust.

Charity. Although tax savings is not the primary goal, it is important to note that transferring wealth to a church, ministry, or other charity is the most tax-efficient choice. Gifts to charity are 100 percent deductible from your estate. Contrasted to leaving money to heirs, your estate would pay no estate tax on the money left to charity.

Let me use an extreme case to illustrate the leverage you can obtain by giving assets to charity. Probably the wealthiest people I know are a married couple who are billionaires. They have no children and plan to leave 100 percent of their estate to charity. They will pay zilch, nada, zero, nothing in federal or state estate and inheritance taxes.

Compare this billion-dollar estate with no taxes to a more modest family in Iowa. Their taxable estate totals $5 million of life insurance, farmland, and IRAs. They have done no planning, just a simple will dividing everything equally among their kids. If the parents die in a car crash tomorrow, their kids will not get $5 million. Nearly $2.3 million will go to the third choice . . .

Government. Most choose the government as a steward unintentionally by paying estate tax that could have been avoided. Do you really want the government to acquire and then distribute the wealth under your control? Unless you choose the next steward, the government will choose it for you. Only the living steward can plan for the distribution of assets through a will and through tax-saving techniques. Rarely does the government have the same objectives for your wealth that you do.

Are there legal and ethical ways to reduce the tax bite from the government? Yes. As we will discuss more in chapter 7, there are tools and techniques to minimize taxes. But they take planning. They require that you first make a choice of the next stewards.

Given the three choices, some wealthy individuals are deciding to select charities—rather than the government or their children. Many make some strange and unfortunate charitable choices:

⊃The newspaper headlines surprised even the wealthy: "$1 Billion Gift to United Nations." Ted Turner, founder of CNN, agreed to give $100 million each year for 10 years for various U.N. causes. The year before, Turner had given $28 million to the Bat Conservation Society, Friends of the Wild Swan, and many other environmental causes.[1]

⊃Gary Comer, the billionaire founder of Lands' End, Inc., has provided millions of dollars to scientists to study global climate change theory. Mr. Comer has funded research trips to find the path of ancient floods after glaciers melted at the end of the Ice Age. He puts up big dollars for scientists to develop new ice-dating techniques and for expeditions in search of evidence of rare tropical glaciers in . . . no kidding . . . Latin America.[2]

⊃Warren Buffet, the famous billionaire investor, is the world's second richest man. Buffett, a long-time supporter of pro-abortion causes, plans to leave his wealth to a foundation that will likely focus on population control issues.

⊃Philanthropic eyebrows were raised when Ruth Lilly, heiress of pharmaceutical company, Eli Lilly, left $100 million to *Poetry* magazine. The sixty-page monthly magazine is relatively unknown with a circulation of only 11,000. Even the editor of the magazine admitted that a gift of this size upon a tiny magazine seemed disproportionate.[3]

Probably you won't choose to give to conserve bats, study ice, or endow small poetry magazines. But what will your choice be? If you've stayed with me this far into the book, you are probably committed to choosing the next steward wisely. I think you will be accountable for your choice of the next steward of His wealth.

Many people choose a local university or perhaps their alma mater. What is God's likely reaction to a decision to leave some of His assets to your alma mater, if it is an institution whose teachings oppose Christianity, when perhaps one or two billion have never heard the good news of Jesus Christ?

WEALTH TRANSFER
DECISION-MAKING PROCESS

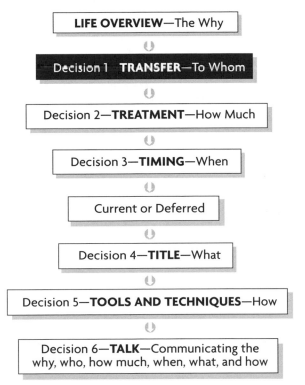

I agree with the urgency of Thomas Monaghan, founder of Domino's Pizza, who has given an estimated $100 million to charity. "A lot of people give money to social causes like fighting poverty or to medical research. These are all very good things, but I don't think they're as important as helping people get to heaven. My overall goal in giving is to save as many souls for the buck as I can."[4]

All of us in America were shocked, angered, and mournful about the terrorist attacks of September 11, 2001. Rightfully so, as nearly three thousand people died on that tragic day. While not minimizing the death of innocent victims in New York, Washington, and Pennsylvania, Rich Stern, president of World Vision, helped me put the death toll in perspective with the global impact of death and suffering around the world. He said that thirty thousand children die *per day* from poverty. He believes that many of those deaths could be eliminated by clean water and good, basic food.

We have incredible wealth in our country while there are incredible needs elsewhere. Would God have us leave His assets to our adult children, who have enjoyed all of life's basic needs, education, recreation, and material blessings, or help some of the thirty thousand children who suffer daily?

The Transfer Decision is the first and most important decision in the wealth transfer process. It drives the other decisions in the process. To whom does the wealth go?

The following three principles can help you make wise choices for the next steward of your wealth. Make your financial and wealth transfer decisions, like your other life decisions, based upon sound principles.

THE TREASURE PRINCIPLE⟿ You can't take it with you, but you can send it on ahead.

I spent most of my working career managing other people's money by evaluating and selecting appropriate investments for them to meet their financial goals. In doing so, I looked for a good return. I looked for investments that would last and tried to avoid investments that may decline in value.

Jesus Christ gave much better investment advice than my firm in His teaching in the "Sermon on the Amount" when He said:

Do not store up for yourselves treasures on earth, where moth and rust destroy, and where thieves break in and steal. But store up for yourselves treasures in heaven, where moth and rust do not destroy, and where thieves do not break in and steal. For where your treasure is, there your heart will be also. (Matthew 6:19–21)

We sometimes miss the fact that Jesus is all for treasures. He simply wants us to store them in the right place: heaven. That's a wise investment.

In his outstanding book called *The Treasure Principle,* Randy Alcorn summarizes this principle: "You can't take it with you—but you can send it on ahead."[5]

Well, how do I get these treasures? The Bible says God is a rewarder, "Behold, I am coming soon! My reward is with me, and I will give to everyone according to what he has done" (Revelation 22:12). He gives us rewards for acts of kindness (Matthew 10:42), for enduring temptation (James 1:12), and for good works (Ephesians 6:8).

Rewards also accrue from generous giving. "Go, sell your possessions and give to the poor, and you will have treasure in heaven" (Matthew 19:21). Jesus also emphasized helping those who can't give you something in return:

Then Jesus said to his host, "When you give a luncheon or dinner, do not invite your friends, your brothers or relatives, or your rich neighbors; if you do, they may invite you back and so you will be repaid. But when you give a banquet, invite the poor, the crippled, the lame, the blind, and you will be blessed. Although they cannot repay you, you will be repaid at the resurrection of the righteous." (Luke 14:12–14)

Can you grasp this powerful concept? What I do on earth can accumulate treasures in heaven that will last forever!

After I gave a speech not long ago, a gentleman came up to me with a compliment. He said, "You know, one of the most profound things you have ever said in a book still has an impact on me. It was 'In terms of your treasure, you are either moving away from it or toward it. Those are your two choices.'" He quoted this, and

I told him that I didn't remember writing it, but it is rather profound.

I believe the gentleman may have had me confused with Randy Alcorn, author and director of Eternal Perspective Ministries. Randy and I have often both given presentations at the same conferences. So, I am not sure I deserved this man's compliment. (No doubt, Dean Martin felt the same way when someone complimented him on his outrageous slapstick comedy or someone complimented Jerry Lewis on his warm baritone voice and dashing looks.)

Randy says it like this:

> Many have stored up their treasures on earth, not in heaven. Each day brings us closer to death. If your treasures are on earth, that means each day brings you closer to losing your treasures. . . . He who lays up treasures in heaven looks forward to eternity; he's moving daily toward his treasures. To him, death is gain. He who spends his life moving away from his treasures has reason to despair. He who spends his life moving toward his treasures has reason to rejoice.[6]

This is why it is so hard for some to write their wills or set up the wealth transfer process. Making those tough decisions, signing those documents, having the family conversations may remind some they are moving away from their treasure. This is why some people really hate to die. They are leaving behind something that is incredibly valuable to them.

That reminds me of a story about a rich man who was near death. He was very grieved because he had worked so hard for all he had and wanted to be able to take it with him to heaven. So he began to pray that he might be able to take some of his wealth with him.

An angel heard his plea and appeared to him. "Sorry, but you can't take your wealth with you."

The man begged the angel to speak to God to see if He might bend the rules. The man continued to pray that his wealth could follow him.

The angel reappeared and informed the man that God had decided to allow him to take one suitcase with him. Overjoyed, the man gathered his largest suitcase, filled it with pure gold bars, and placed it beside his bed.

Soon afterward, he died and showed up at the gates of heaven. The angel at the gates saw the suitcase and said, "Hold on, you can't bring that in here!"

The man explained to the angel that he had permission and asked him to verify his story with God.

Sure enough, the angel checked it out, came back, and said, "You're right. You are allowed one carry-on bag, but we're supposed to check its contents before letting it through."

The angel opened the suitcase to inspect the worldly items that the man found too precious to leave behind and exclaimed, "What?!? You brought pavement?"

As believers, we are leaving something behind that has no value. We are moving toward something that has eternal value.

From our discussion so far, you may think that I am implying you should leave all your money to mission work or a charity and none to your kids. I am not saying that. Please understand that I am simply recommending that you think through, pray over, and consider your decisions in a process. Remember, not deciding is a decision.

Giving to charity is one way, but not the only way, to gain treasures in heaven. Actually, God doesn't need the money. What God wants is the use of His money in productive ways. Maybe a productive way is buying that dresser for your wife, taking that vacation to build a memory, or paying off that debt to give you financial freedom.

Jesus said, "If you have not been trustworthy in handling worldly wealth, who will trust you with true riches? And if you

WEALTH TRANSFER
DECISION-MAKING PROCESS

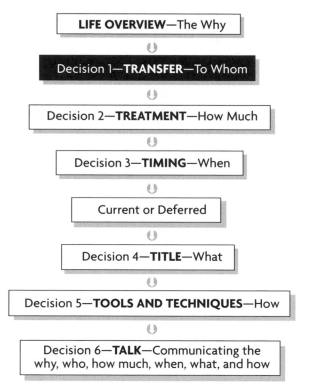

LIFE OVERVIEW—The Why

Decision 1—**TRANSFER**—To Whom

Decision 2—**TREATMENT**—How Much

Decision 3—**TIMING**—When

Current or Deferred

Decision 4—**TITLE**—What

Decision 5—**TOOLS AND TECHNIQUES**—How

Decision 6—**TALK**—Communicating the
why, who, how much, when, what, and how

have not been trustworthy with someone else's property, who will give you property of your own?" (Luke 16:11–12).

You may conclude that your children should get all of your wealth. That is fine. But you should *decide* to do so. Understand the implications of *choosing and preparing* them to be the next stewards of your wealth instead of leaving everything to them by default or simply doing what everyone else does. To help make these decisions, God has given you an in-house consultant if you are married to a Christian spouse. This leads us to the next principle.

THE UNITY PRINCIPLE ⊃ Your spouse completes you, not competes with you.

I remember hearing that the trouble with many women is that they get all excited about nothing—and then they marry him. Howard Hendricks first told me the phrase behind the Unity Principle. In Howie's words, "God did not give you a spouse to frustrate you but to complete you." He helped me see that Judy and I can make better decisions together than either one of us can alone. King Solomon, who had some wisdom about money and wives in his early years, said the following:

Two are better than one,
because they have a good return for their work:
If one falls down,
his friend can help him up.
But pity the man who falls
and has no one to help him up!
Also, if two lie down together, they will keep warm.
But how can one keep warm alone?
Though one may be overpowered,
two can defend themselves. (Ecclesiastes 4:9–12)

My personal experience with my wife, and my observation of other couples, is that we have different strengths and weaknesses. Marriage brings about a challenging but complementary blend of emotions and logic, estrogen and testosterone.

When you are making these decisions related to wealth transfer, unity is necessary between husband and wife. If at first you don't succeed, keep talking, keep listening, keep compromising, and keep praying together.

You keep processing these decisions until you come to an answer. You may need a temporary plan in place while you work out a better plan. Frankly, Judy and I have found we process these decisions for years because circumstances change. Kids start careers, marriages occur, grandkids arrive, divorces may happen. Judy and I find ourselves reassessing whether we have still made the right decisions. It's not always comfortable or easy, but it's necessary for us to agree.

How does a lack of unity raise its ugly head? I see it regularly in comments like these . . .

He Says . . .	She Says . . .
"I don't want that worthless son-in-law to get one penny of our money."	"Think about what this will do to our grandchildren."
"We have enough. Our kids have enough. Let's give more of our wealth to missions."	"My grandfather left me this money. I get to do what I want, and I want to keep it in the family."
"I want to take care of you if I die first, but I don't want your future husband to take money meant for our kids."	"I want to have enough to live on comfortably if you die before me."
"I built this business for the past thirty years. Junior helped me while the others were 'finding themselves' in college. I want him to have it."	"But you can't blame the girls for not wanting to work in a machine shop. We wanted them to get advanced degrees."
"Please attend the planning meeting next week with our advisers to go over our wills."	"Oh, I trust you. I don't care to know all that business and financial stuff. I have other things to do."

If you continue to have difficulty in reaching an agreement, you may benefit from an adviser, such as a financial planner or an attorney, to facilitate the discussions. I would strongly urge you to seek one of the many competent Christian planners to help you process these decisions. Just as you would likely seek a family counselor or a marriage counselor who approaches his practice with a biblical and Christian worldview, you should also use the services of a Christian financial or legal professional. Refer to page 212 for more information about one source of such professionals in the Christian Financial Professionals Network.

Men often initiate and guide much of the wealth transfer process. When they are seeking the Lord's will, this is appropriate because of the leadership and provision they are responsible for. Considering the demographic realities, women should also have a keen interest. Recent statistics show that 90 percent of all women will be single at some point in their lives—either from choosing to remain single, divorce, or death of their spouse.[7] A wife has a vested interest in her husband's planning because statistically she will be on the receiving end of the plans. Often, the wife becomes the widow who must cope with life alone. But no matter who is left, the husband or the wife, it's better to have an agreed-upon financial plan to guide you the rest of your lives.

Dave, a successful business owner, didn't agree with his wife, Sue, about how much to give to their adult children. She felt like their wealth would ruin the children. They hadn't agreed on how much should be divided between charity, children, and the surviving spouse.

Dave left for work one day and didn't return. He died from a massive heart attack at the office. The adult children did receive immediate and substantial inheritances. They quickly wasted it and ventured into immoral lifestyles. Sue was very angry with her deceased husband because she had to live through the gut-wrenching decisions her children made. She watched money being wasted that she could have lived on or given to charity. Not only did Dave and Sue violate the Unity Principle, but they also suffered from not heeding the Wisdom Principle . . .

WEALTH TRANSFER
DECISION-MAKING PROCESS

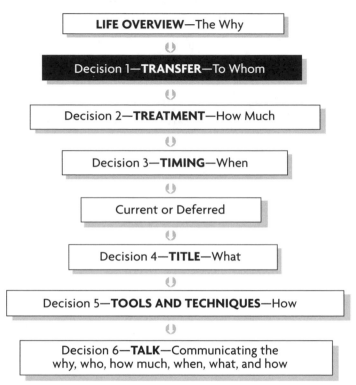

THE WISDOM PRINCIPLE ➲ Transfer wisdom before wealth.

Wealth never creates wisdom. Wisdom may create wealth. If you pass wisdom to your children, you probably can pass wealth to them. If they have enough wisdom, then they may not need your wealth.

Too often in our culture, the attitude of the parents is "I'll take care of the money. You kids just stay in school or play the piano or play soccer." I strongly urge you to reconsider this philosophy. With each passing year, you can pass on more practical experience and needed knowledge about handling money. Don't make money mysterious or a factor in controlling your children and making yourself seem powerful in their lives. You will actually have more influence (God's gentle version of power and control) over their behavior if you teach them how and why your family handles money as it does. The worst thing you can do is to pass wealth if you haven't passed wisdom.

The Bible says, "An inheritance quickly gained at the beginning will not be blessed at the end" (Proverbs 20:21). In biblical times, sons inherited their fathers' properties and thus provided for the rest of their families. What is not so obvious is that, in most instances, the sons received their inheritances while their fathers were still living, enabling the fathers to oversee their sons' stewardship.

In turn, the sons, particularly the oldest, inherited great responsibility for providing for the parents and extended family. Would you be more interested in training your children to handle money wisely if you knew that one day your estate would be in your children's hands and you would have to depend on them for your support?

Good stewardship includes not only providing for your family, but also being sure that every family member knows how to manage that provision. It's so easy to procrastinate. It's a "tyranny of the urgent" problem that keeps us from doing the important items.

In the book, *Wealth to Last*, which I co-authored with Larry Burkett, we related a story about a wealthy businessman seeking counsel. He had been very successful financially and had a sizable estate. When asked what he planned to do with it all, he replied, "I'll leave it to my children, I guess."

Larry then asked him why he didn't just give it to them right then, and he replied, "Why, they don't know how to handle money. They'd just lose it all!"

Becoming a bit bolder, Larry ventured, "Do you think they would lose it after you died as well?"

The businessman responded, "Well, I'll be gone then, so who cares?"

71

I think you should care. God cares. Because being a good steward doesn't have to stop with death.

THE THREE 3'S

In making the transfer decision, we have learned there are three choices (heirs, charity, and government) and three principles (treasure, unity, and wisdom). To help you further, I would recommend asking yourself three questions as you consider transferring wealth.

1. What is the worst thing that can happen if I transfer wealth to _____?
2. How serious is it?
3. How likely is it to occur?

You can also ask these three questions in a more positive frame of mind, such as "What is the best thing that can happen if I transfer wealth to _____?"

In preparing our wealth transfer plans, Judy and I have gone through these questions. We asked them for each aspect of our plans, whether it involved a child, a grandchild, or charity. They are not easy questions to answer, but they are necessary questions to answer if you are trying to pass wealth responsibly.

A friend, very concerned about being a good steward, shared that he was struggling with how much wealth to transfer to his grandchildren compared to mission organizations. His adult children did not need the money. His grandchildren, now young adults, had shown themselves to be very irresponsible with money.

So, I asked him the question: What is the worst thing that can happen if you transfer wealth to your grandchildren?

He replied, "God's resources would be wasted."

I followed up, "How serious is that?"

After reflecting for a minute, he answered, "That's very serious."

"OK," I continued. "So, you say it's a very serious matter that God's resources would be wasted. How likely is that to occur?"

Without a moment's hesitation, he said, "Knowing them, one hundred percent."

I then asked the same questions from the positive and negative perspective of transferring his wealth to mission organizations. Considering and answering these questions helped him to crystallize his thinking, remove false guilt, and feel confident about his plans to fund missionary work.

Such a plan takes courage. Do you have the courage to not leave all your assets to your children? It's challenging to dare to be different from most people in the United States. If you do choose to leave some to your children, do you have the courage to treat them uniquely? The three questions presented in this chapter also can be used for our next decision: The Treatment Decision.

WHAT IF...

Your spouse was asked the following questions: Do you know about your wealth transfer plans? Are you comfortable with them?

WHAT IF...

You inherited one million dollars
when you were eighteen years old.
Thinking back to the way you were as an
eighteen-year-old, how would you have
likely spent the inheritance? What lessons
would you have not learned in life because of
the money (by not having to work as hard, by
not enduring a bit of discomfort or by delayed
gratification)? What accomplishments
would you have not made? What people
might you have not met? What ad-
dictive or sinful lifestyle behaviors might you have been
attracted to?

MAY I ASK A FOLLOW-UP QUESTION?

Q. *Ron, I agree with the principle of passing wisdom before wealth, but my children are already grown. Is it too late? How do I pass wisdom along now?*

A. Certainly, the most formative training period is while your children are young and under your care. It's not too late though. Here are some practical ideas...

➲ Share with them some of the financial decisions you are now making and why.

➲ Consider giving a token inheritance now so that you can test them and be available for help and supervision.

➲ Talk with them about some of the financial lessons you have learned. For example, you may have learned a lesson about investing. Share that with them. Let them benefit from your experience.

➲ Locate professional advisers and counselors for them. Perhaps you can pay for the appointments. Your adult children may not have major problems, but they may benefit from a financial planning session, personality/ self-awareness testing from a counselor, or a meeting with a lawyer.

➲ If you own a business, involve your children in the significant decisions of the business. Even if they do not work in the business, consider making them members of the board of directors or give them a small amount of ownership to let them see the overall operations. Share with them why you are making certain decisions.

➲ Involve your adult children in the giving decisions you are making now and for the future. If you have a special missions interest, invite them and pay for them to participate in mission trips, conferences, or conventions of ministries you support. If you have a foundation, let them participate.

JUST DO IT RIGHT!

FIGHTING THE GOOD FIGHT
IN THE BUSINESS WORLD

Arthur and Lewis Tappan, brothers, business innovators, and evangelical leaders in the 1800s, are relatively obscure names today. They are early examples of using God's resources provided through business to fund His working in the world.

Arthur Tappan began a revolutionary style of merchandising after the War of 1812. He bought large shiploads of merchandise and resold his goods wholesale to country merchants. Because he demanded cash or very short-term notes and traded in huge volumes, he offered competitively low prices to rural storeowners.

Making significant profits, Arthur hired his brother to help him use the company's profits for Christian causes. They saw their business as the means to fund and manage various evangelical societies that distributed Bibles, tracts, and Sunday school materials.[8]

Not afraid of negative public relations, the Tappans founded the Magdalene Society, which ministered to the fallen women of New York City. This angered some of New York's elite wealthy, who owned brothels and theaters where prostitutes met their clients. The Tappans again angered business leaders when they used company profits to organize a campaign against delivery of U.S. mail on Sunday. Lewis Tappan said, "When we saw the heathen against us, we had evidence of the righteousness of the cause."[9]

In the early 1830s, the brothers saw a larger moral issue looming in America: the expansion of the slave economy in the south. The Tappans tapped their company to help William Lloyd Garrison found the American Anti-Slavery Society. From the company headquarters, the Tappans spearheaded fund-raising drives for the antislavery movement, sponsored speakers and revivalists, and organized national postal campaigns.

They organized an evening church service of black and white worshippers, defying the strict segregationist rules of the time. A riot followed and the Tappans nearly lost their lives. As they further gathered support for the cause, Lewis Tappan's household furniture was burned in the street and rioters vandalized the iron-shuttered company store. The Tappans didn't see this as a loss but as more publicity and attention to their antislavery principles.

The Tappans' merchandising business began to wane, threatening the pipeline of funds for the growing antislavery movement in the north. Arthur, facing fatigue and depression, tried unsuccessfully to keep the merchandising business afloat. Sensing that God ruled his fortune and his heart, Lewis began another business to maintain a cash flow. Lewis walked through lower Manhattan daily to obtain storekeeper subscribers to his new credit rating agency.

Resident agents, usually attorneys, would inform Lewis's office of the financial reliability of small-town merchants. At his various offices, Tappan's clerks would read from huge ledgers the reports about specific storeowners to inquiring subscribers. If a country storekeeper defaulted on its obligations, Tappan's contract lawyers (Abraham Lincoln was one) would sue on behalf of the city subscribers.[10]

This new profitable business operation allowed the Tappans to continue to support their causes, including the *Amistad* prisoners. National attention focused on the horrors of the slave trade after the floundering ship in the Atlantic was boarded by the U.S. Navy. A group of Mendi Africans overthrew the crew of the Cuban slave ship, *L'Amistad,* to protest their treatment by slave traders and owners. What the U.S. Navy saw confirmed their ill treatment. However, the Africans were still taken into custody. While lengthy court hearings and debate over the fate of the *Amistad* prisoners continued, Lewis Tappan shared the gospel with them, provided for them, and retained former President John Quincy Adams to argue their case before the U.S. Supreme Court.

Adams won the case. Although Adams gets more credit in Steven Spielberg's 1998 film *Amistad*, Adams wrote to Lewis

Tappan, "The Captives are free! But thanks, thanks in the name of humanity and justice to you."[11] Tappan arranged for the Mendi Africans to return to their homeland so they could spread the gospel of Jesus to their fellow countrymen.

Lewis Tappan later sold his national credit rating agency at a handsome profit so he could devote his full-time efforts to his calling in the antislavery movement. Eventually, Tappan's firm became the R. G. Dun Company. It later merged with Bradstreet, a competitor. Today, Dun and Bradstreet, a multi-billion dollar company, is the leading provider of business information to other businesses.

From the proceeds of the sale, Lewis Tappan founded the *Amistad* Committee to spread antislavery information to other countries. As the antislavery movement succeeded with the ending of the Civil War, the name and purpose of the *Amistad* Committee was later changed to the American Missionary Association. The AMA developed missions in West Africa, East Asia, the British West Indies, and other locations. It founded and operated colleges and schools for the southern freed people, such as Fisk University (Nashville), Berea College (Kentucky), and Howard University (Washington).

"And that's why you should
trust me with all your money."

Stu's Views

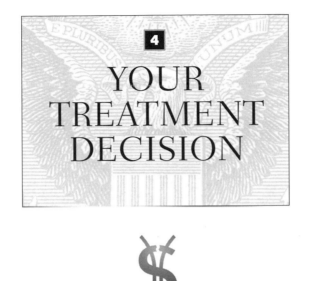

YOUR
TREATMENT
DECISION

Probably every parent of more than one child feels the same way. How can children coming from the same two parents, with the same gene pool, living in the same environment, with the same stimuli be so different? Judy and I are amazed at how our five children have such different personalities and approaches to life.

Then, as children become adults, their paths of life often differ. As I was working on this chapter, my grandson Jack came bounding into my office, giving me a welcome interruption. Judy and I watch him regularly for our daughter Karen. This energetic two-year-old soon had his oversized, lightweight, extra-bouncy ball flying all over my office.

Sadly, Karen is a single mom recovering from an unexpected divorce and seeking just what she will do with her life. When Judy and I revised our wills recently, we gave specific and deliberate thought to how we may provide for Karen and Jack compared

WEALTH TRANSFER DECISION-MAKING PROCESS

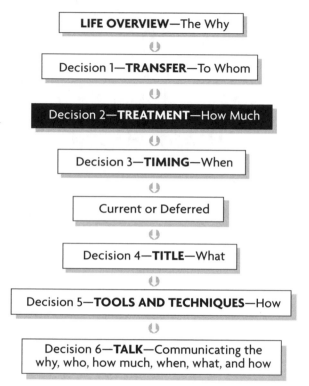

to our other children and grandchildren. We believe that we should be available to help Jack and Karen with babysitting and some financial assistance. We don't have to provide exactly the same for another child, such as our son who is an attorney.

THE UNIQUENESS PRINCIPLE ⮞ Love your children equally and as such treat them uniquely.

Is such treatment unfair? We don't think so. Our approach to the second decision, the Treatment Decision, in our wealth transfer process is based on the Uniqueness Principle: *Love your children equally and as such treat them uniquely.*

To do otherwise would dishonor them. Sons are different from daughters, sons-in-law are different from daughters-in-law, grandchildren are different from other grandchildren. You may have heard it said that the greatest inequality is treating unequal people equally.

As you contemplate choosing the next steward of God's wealth, you may realize that some of your children are much better equipped to handle wealth than others. You may reflect upon your family situation and realize that some have more genuine needs than others. Love them unconditionally, but treat them uniquely. They are unique in their character, values, ability to deal with life; unique in their vocation, health, and immediate family situation.

I believe that a parent should consider differences in children —differences due to age, gender, temperament, their demonstrated ability to handle money, their spiritual commitment, their spiritual maturity, their known or unknown marriage partners, and their children. It is a parent's and grandparent's responsibility to entrust God's resources to children only if they have demonstrated the ability to handle those resources in a manner that would be pleasing to Him who is the owner of all.

If a parent entrusts God's resources to a slothful child, it's no different from giving those resources to any slothful stranger. The fact that because you have a child should not make the child the automatic beneficiary of your estate. If we leave money to someone to whom we have not left wisdom, it can be a devastating situation and may not be an example of good stewardship. I believe that much prayer, wisdom, and courage are needed in making the Treatment Decision. Obviously, great emotion and perhaps tradition are involved. This is why you ultimately must talk with your family about your decisions. It's better to discuss unequal distributions to children while you are alive than to run the risk of bitterness toward you, or toward each other, after you are dead.

Karen's unanticipated divorce resulted in emotional and financial needs very different from her brothers and sisters. So, we have helped her uniquely with her unique needs. We never felt it was unfair to treat her uniquely. For example, if we gave her three hundred dollars to help with her expenses, then we didn't have to write a three-hundred-dollar check to each of our other children.

Over time, circumstances may change and that may warrant a change in our wealth transfer plans. What if Karen marries a wealthy doctor? What if she becomes a missionary to Africa? Wouldn't these changes in circumstances perhaps alter how Judy and I transfer wealth to Karen and Jack? Or, maybe she'll struggle for years as a single mom trying to juggle earning an income and raising a child and our plans will remain the same.

BUT TREATING OUR CHILDREN
DIFFERENTLY DOESN'T FEEL RIGHT

I acknowledge that this is a hard decision to process. If you have more than one child, then it can feel unfair at first. So, let's examine this notion of fairness further.

As parents, we work hard to avoid favoritism. Rightfully so, as favoritism has caused much pain and divisiveness in families for thousands of years. Look at the story of Joseph in the Old Testament. The Bible says that his father, Jacob, "loved Joseph more than any of his other sons" (Genesis 37:3). Jacob later gave Joseph a richly ornamented coat of many colors.

Although Jacob had unique treatment toward Joseph, Jacob violated the Uniqueness Principle. Jacob did not love his sons equally. Treat children uniquely, yes, but such treatment should come from a base of equal love. Because Jacob showed favoritism (like his father Isaac had shown to Jacob's brother Esau), the unique treatment of the coat became a symbol and lightning rod of conflict with Joseph's brothers.

To avoid a *perception* of unequal love, you must communicate with all of your adult children. That is why the Talk Decision (which we will discuss further in chapter 8) is important. I have observed that distributing money will likely generate some emotions. Money has a symptomatic power about it—it brings out in people and families symptoms of problems that lie underneath. Curiously, the more money is being distributed, the more intense the symptoms. Money aggravates these family problems and is *not* the magic cure that people imagine it to be.

When parenting young children, you do have to be concerned with their perceptions of fairness. They do not understand reasons for giving. If you go away on a business trip and bring a gift for only one of your three children, then they will perceive that you have different amounts of love. That would be cruel. This is why most parents of young children go to great lengths to treat them equally. Our society takes this fairness so far that even when bringing a gift to a newborn baby most people will also bring a gift to the three-year-old brother.

Many parents continue these legalistic notions of exact fairness to adult children. However, adult children can understand subtle distinctions of why an act of generosity to another adult child may be appropriate or convenient. They wouldn't necessarily expect the same, but you may need to communicate the reasons behind your actions to help them understand.

Consider the Smiths and their twins, Joe and John. Joe excelled at school and sports. With an engaging personality and godly character, Joe became a successful engineer, committed father, and faithful husband. John, on the other hand, was born with a slight physical handicap and learning disability. He obtained his high school diploma at age twenty-five and works at a government-subsidized program for the disadvantaged.

The Smiths spent a much larger portion of their resources on John than on Joe to pay for medical bills, research, special testing, modifications to their home, special equipment, tutoring, and custodial care. The Smiths have also planned to transfer wealth to a trust to provide for John in the future if they die before him.

They told Joe of their plans. As they expected, Joe understood and wholeheartedly endorsed his parents' plans for his special-needs brother. Joe didn't need his parents' money. They had given him all he needed to do well in life.

Unfortunately, not all adult children are as mature as Joe. Many children play the so-called "fairness" issue to make the parents feel guilty. Even when a will contains an equal division, fairness issues may arise. Just imagine the following being said with an edge, a bit of a whine, and an intent to place guilt.

> ➲ "He went to an expensive private college. I went to a community college. You should pay the difference and put a down payment on my house."
> ➲ "You paid for her wedding, but I am not married. That's not fair."
> ➲ "I never caused you any trouble, but my brother has been in rehab after rehab. When do I get my fair share?"
> ➲ "You loaned money to his business that later went bankrupt. I should hope he is having that deducted from his inheritance."

Many older people just want peace in their family. So, they don't even think through the wealth transfer decisions and "just divide everything equally among the kids." As the above quotes illustrate, even the so-called approach of "equal shares" can bring about the same arguments the parents hoped to prevent.

REMEMBER YOU ARE THE STEWARD AND ACCOUNTABLE TO GOD

Sometimes as parents of young children it seemed our kids ruled the roost. We had to stop at those times and say to ourselves, "Wait, we're in charge here."

The same idea applies to your stewardship. *You* are a steward of God's resources on His behalf. You are *not* a steward of your children's resources. You are *not* accountable to your children about how you transfer or spend His money. *You are* accountable to God.

Certainly, you want to promote harmony in your family, you would not want to cause your family members to stumble, and you want to lovingly communicate your desires. But ultimately you must resist the emotional manipulation that some adult children will attempt. I have observed this many times when one of the kids seems to know the right emotional buttons to push with his widowed mother.

You may have to show tough love to your adult children. To help you make your Treatment Decision, I would suggest using again the three questions presented in the last chapter. Ask these in respect to each child.

1. What is the worst (or best) thing that can happen if I transfer wealth to _____?
2. How serious is it?
3. How likely is it to occur?

Let me illustrate with the Drake family. The Drakes are amazed at the different values that their grown children have displayed—even though they all *say* they are Christians. Carol, the oldest, married a lawyer with a successful practice. They belong to the right country club, live in the right neighborhood, and drive the right cars. Carol and her husband are far more concerned about material items and wealth than the Drakes ever were.

The middle Drake child, Josh, has far more spiritual commitment and fervor than the Drakes ever had. He graduated from seminary with advanced degrees, and he works at starting new churches in the inner city. Despite his education and talents, Josh earns very little salary. He and his team are very effective at their ministry, but their organization has difficulty raising funds from other churches that don't share the same passion for inner-city ministry.

The youngest Drake child, Rick, was the brightest and most naturally gifted of all their children. However, Rick's occasional experiments with drugs, his tendency toward laziness, and his failed marriages have left him living alone in a trailer. Despite having had several good business ideas, he always seems to find a way to mess them up. He spends most of his time watching cable TV rather than finding a better-than-minimum-wage job.

As the Drakes began thinking of how to transfer their modest wealth, they applied the three questions. After analyzing them further and seeing their answers on paper, it was clear that any money left to Carol, the oldest, or Rick, the youngest, would only tilt their lives further out of balance. The Drakes felt that the best stewardship of God's resources would be for Josh to receive the majority of their wealth.

The Drakes had to fight against those feelings of being unfair. But during a peaceful family get-together they explained their rationale to their adult children. They blessed each of their children verbally and expressed their love to them. To the parents' surprise, all of the children agreed that their plan made sense. Even more pleasant and surprising to the Drakes, they began to notice over time that Carol and Rick began to make gradual improvements in their value systems. Each of them also began supporting Josh's ministry after hearing of the funding challenges.

After prayerfully considering your situation and evaluating the three questions presented earlier, you may end up treating your children all equally. That's fine. But if you do, you will have done so as a conscious decision. A good steward should think through the possible ramifications as opposed to just defaulting into a decision.

The benefit—and perhaps the frustration—of this book is that I am not telling you the answers. Instead, I am presenting a process for you to think through the questions for your situation. Many people have asked me how to write their will. I always make it a practice to ask, "What are you really trying to accomplish?" Ask God to lead you to the best decision He wants. Sometimes the answer may be surprising—like when I was asked a difficult question after a speaking engagement.

A doctor and his wife approached me. They had three children, including a son who was involved in an immoral lifestyle in Hollywood. The couple had heard me speak about these issues of wealth transfer. In the interest of what they thought was "good stewardship," they had all but decided to leave the wayward child out of their wills. Giving him a large inheritance, they reasoned, would be tantamount to wasting God's resources.

The only problem was that they did not feel comfortable about the decision. They had prayed about it and sought the advice of several wise and mature Christians, yet they still struggled emotionally with the idea of disinheriting their son. They asked me what I thought they should do. (It's easy for me to give out advice until people follow it; then it becomes scary!)

I immediately breathed a quick prayer: "Lord, help!" As they related their situation, I was asking myself, *What's the worst thing that can happen?* The answer was that some money could be wasted. That is serious. But the best thing that can happen is that he may return to Christ. Then, prompted by the Holy Spirit, I asked the couple a few questions. "Do you believe that God owns it all?"

"Yes," they said. "We think God is the owner and we are the stewards."

Then, I asked a more pointed question: "Would your son be more likely to repent and come to Christ if (a) he were sitting in the attorney's office learning he is disinherited, and understood why, or (b) if you were to include him in your inheritance?"

The couple thought about it and talked about it. "We think if he were disinherited then he would never ever consider the gospel again. He'd be more likely to come to Christ if he were in our will. Mercy tends to soften him more than tough discipline. But our assets belong to God—we can't just use them to benefit our son, can we?"

Instead of answering that question, I asked another one: "Do you think God has enough money to spend on your son's potential salvation?"

They said, "Well, yeah, that's nothing."

"Now, what's the best thing that can happen to him from a spiritual, eternal standpoint? Don't you think God would approve of your stewardship decision to leave your son an inheritance if it would encourage him to become a Christian?"

I could see the light dawn in their eyes. "Yes," they said, "He would." And with that, it became an easy decision. They would include their son in their wills.

They knew their son best. They weren't trying to buy him salvation but to keep open the path to Christ. In their case, I think they made a good stewardship decision. They chose to use the money in the possibility that he may come to Christ.

This example puts into perspective the wealth transfer process. You may tend to get legalistic and rigid. Sometimes, though, you can be too close to an issue, emotionally speaking, to think clearly and ask the right questions. When that happens, it is important to pray diligently for God's direction, work through this process of thinking and decision making, and seek professional counsel from a Christian perspective.

The first two decisions of "to whom?" (transfer) and "how much?" (treatment) pave the way for the next decision of "when?" (timing).

WHAT IF...

You left an equal, significant inheritance to each of your adult children. What if you were able to peer into their lives five years from now? How might the inheritance have affected each one? Would you be pleased with your decision to treat them equally?

MAY I ASK A FOLLOW-UP QUESTION?

Q. *One of our three children has frequently been overbearing, intimidating, and adversarial in many dealings with his siblings and us. Because of his choices in life and his previous wasting of money we have given him, we are planning on leaving him less than the others. We are afraid, however, that he will contest our will. We would not want our estate to incur additional legal costs or have our other children dragged through a messy legal battle. What can we do to limit a possible contesting of the will?*

A. First, I would recommend talking to him about your plans. Many times a will contest occurs as a response—a reaction—after being surprised about not receiving as much as expected. So, build the proper expectations. It may even help him change some behaviors now. Few will contests occur when the reduced or cutout heir knows in advance and why.

Still, the world has plenty of attorneys who will take will contest cases on a contingency basis. Although I am not a lawyer, you can put in place practical defenses to prevent messy lawsuits against your estate and among other children. Most will contest lawsuits try to show you were not of sound mind, you were coerced, or you simply made a mistake. You may include a provision in your will that if any of the heirs try to contest your will then they lose any inheritance provided in the will. Videotape the "signing of the will" and describe what you're doing and why to show you are of sound mind, are competent and rational, and are not under duress. For further proof, schedule an annual physical with your family doctor so your medical records would show you were thinking clearly when you signed the will.

Q. *You mainly spoke about the Treatment Decision as it applies to adult children. What about grandchildren? Does the same Uniqueness Principle apply?*

A. Yes, apply the same process of thinking to grandchildren. Rather than defaulting to the "easy" decision of leaving wealth equally to grandchildren, consider their needs. Are there special needs of one grandchild that may warrant unique treatment?

The increase in the number of family members may make this decision more complex. For example, what if one grandchild's other set of grandparents have already left a substantial amount to that grandchild while another of your grandchildren may not receive anything currently or later from their other set of grandparents?

JUST DO IT RIGHT!

He's Not Chicken
to Make Tough Decisions

Chick-fil-A, the fast-food restaurant known for its chicken sandwiches, is known for its unique approach to business. Its founder, Truett Cathy, has maintained a policy of closing on Sundays to honor the Sabbath. The company gives scholarships to its workers for their education. Rather than the latest action movie, the company uses character-building prizes in its children's meals. Its advertising stops traffic and turns heads with a three-dimensional billboard campaign with cows painting messages to urge Americans to "Eat mor chickin."

The official company Website states the company's values:

> Yet, from the beginning, the first priority for Truett and Chick-fil-A has never been just to serve chicken. It's to serve a higher calling. Our official statement of corporate purpose says that we exist "to glorify God by being a faithful steward of all that is entrusted to us and to have a positive influence on all who come in contact with Chick-fil-A."[1]

Chick-fil-A's results also stand out from the crowd of the competitive fast-food industry. Its 1,100 stores have generated an unprecedented thirty-five-year streak of consecutive sales growth since its beginning in 1967. With annual sales of approximately $1.4 billion, it is one the largest privately owned restaurant chains in the U.S.[2]

Truett Cathy has operated restaurants for almost sixty years. Now in his eighties, he continues to work in the business. But he had to make a decision several years ago about how to pass over the operation of Chick-fil-A. He has three children, two sons who have worked in the company and a daughter who has served in Brazil as a missionary.

Truett made the decision to select one of his sons as the "heir-apparent." Knowing that both sons could not be the main chief, he began to groom one of them for the chief executive officer's role. Truett, in an example of the Wisdom Principle, has spent considerable resources using professional counselors and consultants to help his family with the dynamics of this decision. Knowing the potential impact, he has extensively talked through these decisions, involved his adult children, and used outside counsel to help the family manage these changes.

"...and *that's* why you need to raise my allowance!"

YOUR
TIMING
DECISION

I n the last chapter, I mentioned the Drake family's challenge of wealth transfer. The Drakes decided to transfer wealth to their middle child's ministry (Transfer Decision) rather than divide it equally among their three adult children (Treatment Decision). After making these two important decisions, the Drakes then have to decide *when* to make that transfer.

What are their options? They could transfer much of their estate after both of them die. This is typical of the "estate planning approach" (see page 38) to make sure the Drakes had enough for their lives. The drawback to this option is that Josh's ministry has critical unfunded needs now. A pledge to include the ministry in a will, which may be twenty to thirty years from being distributed, offers little help now.

Or, the Drakes could give substantial resources now. That would be great for ministry now, but would the Drakes have enough to live on?

WEALTH TRANSFER
DECISION-MAKING PROCESS

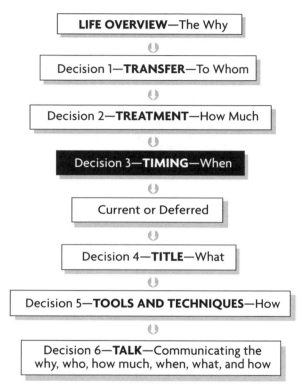

The third option is to do both: Give some currently and some deferred through a will.

How do they decide the proper balance? This same question applies to other situations. Let's say a widow, after prayerfully considering the wealth transfer process, decided to give her wealth to her adult children equally. Should she give it now—when they could use it the most—or give it later?

To help achieve the right balance, I recommend basing your timing decision on the following two principles:

THE KINGDOM PRINCIPLE ⊃ Time your wealth transfer to maximize its use by you, your heirs, and kingdom servants.

THE GIVIN' WHILE LIVIN' PRINCIPLE ⊃ Do your givin' while you're livin' so you're knowin' where it's goin'.

These principles often work together. They apply to timing decisions for wealth transferred to charities or to adult children or grandchildren. Let's say that you have been active in supporting a ministry through your volunteer efforts for many years. Let's further assume you have enough wealth to last your lifetime and you plan to give a substantial gift to the ministry upon your death as mentioned in your will.

The ministry has a current need to complete an obvious God-directed mission. By waiting to give (through your will) until after you die, you may outlive the usefulness of that ministry and your gift may not be needed as much later as it is now. By applying the Kingdom Principle and Givin' While Livin' Principle, you may choose to make substantial gifts now instead of later.

The same principles may apply to your heirs. They may have more need for your inheritance now—to allow a young mother to stay at home, to pay off student loans, or to replace an aging car—instead of when they are fifty or sixty. Although this may sound logical, many people choose to postpone their giving. Why? They have "enough" problems. (I know, you probably think you have enough problems already, but let me explain about "enough" problems.)

How Much Is Enough?

In my early years of financial planning, I observed that the same financial questions I had been asking in my own life were being asked by others as well: missionaries, affluent Africans, poor Africans, full-time Christian workers, successful American executives, pastors, and friends:

⊃ Will I ever have enough?

➲Will it continue to be enough?

➲How much is enough?

Most people, particularly as they get older, fear not having enough money to last them during their lifetimes "in case something happened." This fear may prevent them from participating in excellent giving opportunities during their lifetimes. The danger is they may hoard and place their faith in a bank account rather the Almighty, Omnipotent Provider.

I encourage people to set a finish line. In terms of income and wealth, determine what is the most you need. Determine the maximum. Set a cap. Decide the limit of your lifestyle. It's important to do this in advance, because as our income and wealth increase we seem to find endless ways to spend or save or invest that money. This pushes the finish line further away.

Most are challenged by my question: How much is enough? After contemplating it, the next question then is usually: How do I compute "how much is enough?" I usually say, "I don't know. It depends." (The usual classic answer to avoid a tough question, right?) Or, I might say, "Well, $30,000 is not enough, but $30 million probably is enough. It is up to you and the Lord to determine anything more precise."

Determining how much is enough to live on is not so much a formula as it is a guard against excess accumulation. Although the target may change over time, the process of trying to determine how much is enough is still helpful. The end result of the process is recognizing that an estimated amount, or a range, is enough.

How much is enough is also a function of these variables:

(1) Your age. The older you are, the less in accumulated assets you may need. If you are already ninety, then you probably don't need to plan on having enough for the next thirty years. But if you are fifty, then the answer changes.

(2) Your health and ability to earn an income from work or

investments. If you are healthy and able to work if you desire, then your stored "enough" may be less than someone who is not healthy enough to work or has limited ability to earn through investments.

(3) The ages of your children. The younger they are, the more you may need to have to provide for them. When my children were young and living at home, all of my wealth and estate was to be transferred to them and my wife upon my death. As they graduated from college and chose a vocation and a spouse, I changed my estate plans because they didn't need as much. If I live to be eighty and my children are in their fifties, then I would suspect they will need less and I will change my plans again.

(4) The needs of your children. If your children or grand-children have significant health problems or life problems, then your "enough" may need to be more than your neighbor's "enough" who has healthy, educated adult children with few problems.

(5) Accomplishing other God-given objectives. You may own a business and have a position of influence that God has uniquely given to you to accomplish His purposes. If so, the value of your business may be very high. But perhaps it is appropriate to retain that to continue accomplishing God's objectives.

May I point out that "How much is enough?" will also vary over time. In one decade, your children may not be doing well and you need to have resources to help. In the next decade, they may all earn more than you ever dreamed of making.

Let me encourage you to think about how your lifestyle finish line can affect your giving. When I ask the question, "How much is enough?" most people immediately start thinking about how much money they need to live on, or to save, or to achieve their long-term goals. These considerations are obviously important—especially as you set your lifestyle finish line—but I want to challenge you to look at the question another way. How much is enough to *give?* Instead of asking yourself how much money you need and then trying to figure out how much you can give out of whatever's left over, flip-flop your perspective. Start by asking yourself how generous you want to be.

Deciding how much to give is not a function of a set formula. Instead the choice is dependent on three levels: how much you *should* give, how much you *could* give, and how much you *would* give. You can reach any and all of these levels. All it requires is that you make a choice and tackle the three levels in sequential order.

Giving level	Biblical description	Amount/ process	Reason
Should give	Tithe	10% of income/ Proportionate	Recognize God's ownership
Could give	Sacrificial	>10% of income/ Planned	Develop discipline, sacrificial mindset
Would give	Faith	% of wealth/ Pre-committed	Experience a life of faith & joy

I have written about the "enough" questions in other books. Then, most recently, I co-authored a book with Larry Burkett addressing this fear of having enough called *Wealth to Last*. My point here is to acknowledge the primary hurdle in applying the Kingdom and Givin' While Livin' Principles and encourage you to work through these "enough" questions. Enough said. Let's explore ways a wise steward approaches giving.

MAKING THE MOST OF YOUR GIVING TO CHARITY

Let me give you three very motivating reasons to give now: (1) The prospect of eternal rewards, (2) the unleashing of God's compounded rates of return, and (3) the uncertainty of the future.

As I pointed out in the Treasure Principle in chapter 3, the

Bible says God is a rewarder. The giving you do on earth will result in eternal rewards. Even the smallest generous action, such as giving a cup of water in Jesus' name (Mark 9:41), merits rewards.

Thinking through the implications of these truths, my own belief is that you get no eternal reward for assets given at death. You don't have any choice. You are leaving it all anyway! How can you receive a reward for something you kept your entire life and were forced to give only at death? God will reward you later for your sacrifices now, for your faith shown now, for your unselfishness now in this life.

Another reason to give now instead of later is to start God's rate of return compounding. During the last few years, the available interest rates on bank certificates of deposit and savings accounts have been very low. During the early 2000s, a depositor could expect rates of only 1 percent or less on savings accounts and 2–3 percent on CDs. The stock market returns during the early years of this century have been negative. Over longer periods of time, the stock market tends to average—not guarantee—between 10–12 percent per year depending on the time frame.

How do these current rates of return compare to God's rate of return? In the Parable of the Sower, Jesus says that He can provide a yield ranging from 3,000 percent to 10,000 percent! He said He can produce a crop of thirty times, sixty times, or one hundred times what was sown (Matthew 13:23).

Any investment adviser would realize that a return of 12 percent, over time, is considered phenomenal. A thirtyfold return means getting something thirty times over—which translates into a 3,000 percent return on an annual basis! Imagine making an investment that promises to grow at 3,000 or 6,000 or 10,000 percent. Now that is truly phenomenal!

Look at the following chart that shows the power of compounding. If you invested a lump sum of $10,000 and earned 6 percent per year, you would have $57,435 after thirty years.

COMPOUNDING				
Time + Money + Yield				
Investing a lump sum of $10,000				
%	**10 years**	**20 years**	**30 years**	**40 years**
6%	$17,908	$32,071	$57,435	$102,857
12%	31,058	96,463	299,599	930,510
24%	85,944	738,641	6,348,199	54,559,126
25%	93,132	867,362	8,077,936	75,231,638

The power of compounding results because interest earns interest, which earns interest, which earns interest, which earns interest, *ad infinitum.* In other words, the amount is not nearly as important as the interest rate and the time period. The earlier you start and the more you earn in interest, *the less you need to start with.*

How important is the time period? Very important—you can see the difference between the amounts available after thirty and forty years.

How important is the interest rate? Look at the chart. At 25 percent, $10,000 grows to $75,231,638 in forty years, but at 24 percent, it only grows to $54,559,126 in the same length of time. Now 24 percent is not a reasonable rate of return available to financial investors, but I use it to illustrate a key point. The 1 percent difference in the rate results in a higher amount of nearly $21,000,000. So, giving now to God's kingdom starts the compounding clock sooner, and His rates beat any others available to you.

I serve as a director of a charitable foundation. Charitable foundations consist of significant assets that are used to fund charitable causes. The directors help to determine how much is given each year to these causes and how the assets are invested to allow continued future giving.

At a recent board of directors meeting, we were discussing the stock market decline and how the foundation assets had dropped dramatically. Several wise investment people serve as employees and directors of this board. Some were saying, "We think over the next two to five years, the market is going to recover at least twenty to thirty percent from its current low levels. Let's reduce the foundation's giving right now and take advantage of the potential twenty to thirty percent growth in the stock market. Then we will have more to give later."

After listening to the discussion, I said, "Let me share something with you. What is God's rate of return? The Bible says it is thirtyfold, sixtyfold, or one-hundredfold. That's a pretty good rate. So, perhaps we should deplete the foundation assets entirely by giving in order to get up to ten thousand percent. That would certainly beat the most optimistic stock market forecasts." This reminder of God's potential returns changed the tone of the board's conversation. In the end, we decided to continue our level of giving instead of reducing it.

Rewards like these are beyond calculation or comprehension. They are not measured by human standards. Yet they are real. The small blessings we see on earth are a mere foretaste of the bounty to come. Jesus says that the return provided to you will be hard to measure, but it will be based on your level of giving, "Give, and it will be given to you. A good measure, pressed down, shaken together and running over, will be poured into your lap. For with the measure you use, it will be measured to you" (Luke 6:38).

I know we can't imagine all of His amazing ways of using us, but consider with me a few scenarios. What if your giving now enables your local church to give a Christian witness or Bible now, and that outreach reaches a young man who becomes an effective evangelist? Perhaps thousands are reached through him because of the timely gift.

Or, consider a gift given now that will allow a ministry to promote itself to a large convention. This opportunity may be a catalyst for hundreds more to get involved and sign up for this ministry.

Why do Christian music artists team with World Vision or Compassion International or other organizations to promote these ministries? Couldn't these artists simply give themselves or leave a significant bequest after they die? Because it's usually better to allow more Christian people to share the vision and the giving. God's compounding affects more than monetary multiplication. It affects Christians' hearts, it involves our mind and energy in God's purposes, and it affects lives for eternity now *and* later.

Whenever a gift is given to kingdom causes, it doesn't just make an impact for that week and then stop. It will still be making an impact twenty to thirty years from now through changed lives and the spreading of the gospel.

Another problem with giving out of your estate—instead of currently—is that you don't know the future. Let's say that Bob made a will in 1985 that said half of his estate will go to free Christian prisoners in the USSR. In 1988, Bob experienced a debilitating stroke, causing him to lose mental capacity. When Bob died in 1996, several years after the Iron Curtain fell in the former Soviet empire, the organizations he named no longer existed.

The future is so hard to predict—even for so-called experts. I was reminded of this when someone passed along to me these "Famous Wrong Predictions":

> *"Computers in the future may weigh no more than 1.5 tons."*
> *Popular Mechanics*, forecasting
> the relentless march of science, 1949

> *"We don't like their sound, and guitar music is on the way out."*
> Decca Recording Co.
> rejecting the Beatles, 1962

> *"Everything that can be invented has been invented."*
> Charles H. Duell, Commissioner,
> U.S. Office of Patents, 1899

"I think there is a world market for maybe five computers."
> Thomas Watson, chairman of IBM,
> 1943

"This 'telephone' has too many shortcomings to be seriously considered as a means of communication. The device is inherently of no value to us."
> Western Union internal memo, 1876

"Stocks have reached what looks like a permanently high plateau."
> Irving Fisher, Professor of Economics,
> Yale University, 1929

"The wireless music box has no imaginable commercial value. Who would pay for a message sent to nobody in particular?"
> David Sarnoff's associates in response
> to his urgings for investment in radio
> in the 1920s

"I'm just glad it'll be Clark Gable who's falling on his face not Gary Cooper."
> Gary Cooper on his decision not to
> take the leading role in *Gone with
> the Wind*

"A cookie store is a bad idea. Besides, the market research reports say America likes crispy cookies, not soft and chewy cookies like you make."
> Response to Debbi Fields' idea of
> starting Mrs. Fields' Cookies

"Louis Pasteur's theory of germs is ridiculous fiction."
> Pierre Pachet, Professor of Physiology
> at Toulouse, 1872

107

"The abdomen, the chest, and the brain will forever be shut from the intrusion of the wise and humane surgeon."

> Sir John Eric Ericksen, British
> surgeon, appointed Surgeon-
> Extraordinary to Queen Victoria, 1873

"$100 million dollars is way too much to pay for Microsoft."

> IBM, 1982

It can be dangerous presuming upon the future. How can you know what the most important needs are to support years from now? If you limit your giving until after you die, then you may be giving to a need that is not nearly as urgent or important as it is now. If you agree that giving currently is often the wiser approach, then how do you decide to whom to give?

Strategic Giving

The head of one of the country's largest Christian charitable organizations surprised me. In his estimation, fully half of all giving is ineffective. "Most people," he says, "give in response to emotional or persistent appeals. Very few of us take the time to check out an organization to see whether the need is justified or whether the group can produce results."

His perspective provides important criteria for "effective" giving. Before you give to an individual, a church, or a ministry, check it out. Ask the tough questions: Do I want to give for strategic reasons—or is my desire simply an emotional response to a particularly poignant appeal? Is the need truly justified? Can this organization (or person) produce the results it is promising?

Imagine getting a call from a stockbroker who wanted you to invest in a particular company. No matter how good the pitch sounded, you would probably ask to see additional information, such as the company's annual report or prospectus. And if you purchased the stock, chances are good that you'd check the progress of your investment on the financial pages at least monthly—if not daily.

By contrast, most of us give by writing a check and then put the matter out of our minds. We don't think much about giving in the first place, and we spend even less time monitoring the progress of our "investment." But like financial investing, strategic giving demands we perform "due diligence." Before we give, we have to do our homework.[1]

My good friend Pat MacMillan, a management consultant and author, has spent more time and energy studying strategic and leveraged giving than anyone I know. I've borrowed some of his great ideas for inclusion here. According to Pat's analysis, effective ministries exhibit certain definable characteristics. As you evaluate giving opportunities to your church, missionaries, Christian organizations, or other charities, evaluate them based on the following questions.

1. Are the leaders marked by godly characteristics? Christian leaders—pastors, missionaries, organization heads, and so forth —should be men and women of character, integrity, and vision. They must be competent and qualified to do their jobs, and they should have a biblically based vision that can be communicated to their donors in clear, measurable terms. Most important, they should have a growing, vibrant relationship with Jesus Christ. If you cannot trust a group's leaders, you should not be giving money to that organization.

2. Is the ministry active in God's "hot spots"? Some well-meaning churches, missionaries, campus workers, and other ministry-oriented Christians develop plans and programs assuming God will bless their good intentions. Others, however, take the time to find out, as Henry Blackaby explains in *Experiencing God,* what

God is doing and where He is working and then align themselves with His purposes.

Peter Wagner, a well-known missiologist and author, points to patterns in world events as evidence of the Holy Spirit's work. When the Iron Curtain fell, for example, Christians saw God move in amazing ways through Communism's former strongholds. Today, China and Latin America are among the world's evangelistic "hot spots." Whether the action is happening in a church across the street or on an international mission field, strategic ministries are working in God's "hot spots."

3. Is the ministry innovative? Strategic ministries often create, experiment, and challenge. Instead of getting bogged down in a routine, they try new methods and ideas—without letting go of their principles or their message. They see things other ministries might not, such as how to turn a short-term opportunity into a vehicle for long-term growth.

They also make mistakes, so if you want your church or organization to be innovative, you need to be willing to tolerate errors. Effective ministries take risks—and when they make mistakes, they don't cover them up. Instead, they use them as a platform for discovery.

4. Is the ministry growing and cooperative? Strategic ministries achieve results. This progress, coupled with the clear vision and sense of purpose communicated by the leaders, motivates donors to invest in and be part of the ministry. Ministry workers are likewise attracted and motivated—which ultimately leads to even greater ministry growth.

In the same vein, strategic ministries are willing to partner with like-minded people and organizations. When the Billy Graham team comes to a city, for example, they don't build an organization to launch their crusades. Instead, they work with existing churches and ministries, pooling the resources of countless committed Christians—and as a result, denominational barriers crumble.

5. *Is the ministry goal-oriented?* Strategic ministries have a clear sense of what God wants them to do and how He wants them to do it. Effective churches, missionaries, and parachurch groups are committed to their goals—regardless of how their actions might be perceived by their members or supporters. While they are open to suggestions, strategic ministries never let funding—or a lack of it—dictate their goals and decisions.

6. *Is the ministry accountable?* Having established goals, strategic ministries hold themselves and their staff accountable to accomplish these objectives. Instead of measuring only the organization's activity level, effective ministries measure progress and results. One well-known family ministry commissioned an outside researcher to measure how the organization was affecting families. Such an independent analysis can stack results against goals to provide an accurate evaluation of ministry effectiveness.

As you evaluate a church or ministry, ask yourself questions: Are the elders or deacons strong enough to hold the leaders accountable? Is there a credible board of directors in place? If you support an individual missionary, who are the people he or she has to report to? Are there checks and balances in place to ensure that their operations have financial integrity?

7. *Is the ministry endorsed by a strong track record?* The best indicator of what a ministry will do is what it has done. Eloquent appeals and effective fund-raising do not always signal effectiveness in ministry. Instead of analyzing an organization's "look" or style of communication, focus on the ministry and the results it has achieved.

How do you find out the answers to these questions? Read a ministry's annual reports and Website. You can request from the organization its annual informational return to the IRS (Form 990). Beyond these basic steps, consider interviewing someone from the board of directors. Ask why he is involved and gives his time. Ask significant donors why they give to that organization.

Watch for "yellow flags" that God often sends to warn us about foolish decisions. You may remember that many years ago a young, articulate, and most sincere young man appeared on the *Tonight Show* with Johnny Carson. This man was raising funds for a new charity to clothe nude horses. To protect the public from this abomination and offensiveness, he founded an organization to cover the private parts of horses.

Most viewers thought he was out to lunch, but many sent checks and pledges to aid the cause. His businessman-like appearance and sincerity resulted in $100,000 in gifts. Later, he confessed that the charity was a hoax to measure the gullibility of the American public. I don't know if he ever returned the money, but his "experiment" did point out that some will support the craziest purposes without any investigation.

Interview the people who have benefited from the services received from the ministry or organization. Check for an open-door policy. Ministries that are willing to display what God is doing through them and invite their donors to celebrate their partnership in bringing Him glory are not ministries that close their headquarters to visitors.

Remember, you won't be doing God's kingdom any favors by giving to any organization that doesn't do well on these questions. Sometimes ineffective ministries need a financial wake-up call to spur them on. Sometimes, too, a once-vital ministry that has fulfilled its original mission may need to shut down or reorient its focus. Your prayerful decision to discontinue support—coupled with a letter or telephone call of gentle explanation—may be the most strategic way you can use your resources.

However, if you sense God's leading away from a certain organization, look for where He's guiding you to give next. Don't curtail your overall giving; just change direction.

Even if an organization or individual is doing a good job meeting a legitimate need, God may want you to reduce your financial support so that others may take your place. Every dollar you give is a dollar that someone else could be giving. Perhaps God wants someone else to step up to the plate and take advantage of the giving opportunity your vacancy would create.

You do not have to assume that your commitment to give to a particular ministry must be a long-term obligation. Instead, take time each year to evaluate your giving. Keep a list of the people and organizations you support, and pray about whether or not you should continue.

After evaluating potential charities, many strategic choices may still exist. How do you evaluate these then? I think you can narrow your choices by giving where your heart is, where you have a passion.

Passionate Giving

After leaving my accounting firm in the late 1970s, I worked for an organization called Leadership Dynamics. One of my consulting assignments was helping Campus Crusade with several projects in Africa. Over a two-year period, I made eleven trips to Africa. God worked in my life and in my heart to develop a love for the African people and the African culture and a passion to help them follow Him. To this day, I have structured much of my giving to African mission organizations, missionaries, and inner-city ministries. That's just where God put me. It certainly doesn't mean everyone should give to African or inner-city causes.

To accomplish God's objectives in many different places, He has given each of us different levels of interest in specific ministry opportunities. What a marvelous unity there is in our diversity within the body of Christ. One may have a burden and a passion for supporting crisis pregnancy centers while another desires to distribute as many Bibles as possible in Russia. Both may be strategic although much different in their objectives.

How do you develop a passion for a particular ministry or cause? Often, your passion originates according to where God has placed you and whom He has brought into your life. If your teenager becomes active in a youth group or a high school ministry, God may lead you to give to that organization. If your church plants a mission church, you might consider becoming part of that effort—either physically or financially. Your life experiences may give you a particular passion for child abuse victims, recovering alcoholics, or divorce recovery. You may have a burden that could only have developed from God placing it there. Go with that.

You will never be able to give to every strategic and effective church, ministry, or missionary. Instead of spreading yourself thin in an attempt to be part of every good work, consider the God-given passions you have. This goes back to the Life Overview we discussed in chapter 2. What are your interests? What "life story" do you want to write with your giving? Also, keep in mind that you will often need to give to other places out of obedience—whether or not you have a passion for it. Sometimes God challenges us to increase selflessness and humility. I remember times He made clear He wanted me to give to a ministry that wasn't on my "list," but He brought it to my mind and attention and wouldn't let go until I gave.

Leveraged Giving

When our giving follows our passion with positive results, we tend to involve ourselves more, give more cheerfully, and encourage others to give. That's leverage! Your personal giving brings

114

in other volunteers and their gifts like the seed in the good soil produced even more seed.

Not only do results signal an effective ministry, they are also a key indicator of efficiency. Efficient ministries are "leveraged": They get results, maximizing their own impact and providing the greatest returns on a donor's financial investment. Your local church may be a very good example of leveraged, efficient ministry in how it impacts your community.

An excellent example of leveraged giving is the *Jesus* film, which chronicles the life and message of Christ. The film has been translated into four hundred languages and seen by well over a billion people—more than 20 percent of the world's population! Based on how the film is currently being used for evangelism, I know that for every dollar given to that effort, ten people will hear the gospel. That is efficiency.

Focus on the Family is another example of leveraging ministry efforts. Its radio program reaches millions all over the world without its hosts or guests traveling all over the world. The Focus on the Family broadcasts have served as a launching pad for many other ministers and ministries through the years.

In the same way, when you give to support a seminary student or a missionary, your giving may go far beyond that initial investment. One trained pastor can impact hundreds, and even thousands, of people in a lifetime of ministry. Moody Bible Institute trains hundreds of students for the ministry, and it doesn't charge tuition to its students so that they can graduate without debt. Donors who believe in the ministry underwrite the tuition with their gifts. That's how leveraged giving works on a practical, powerful level.

"Matching" programs, too, can significantly leverage your giving. If your employer offers to match your charitable contributions, take advantage of the opportunity. Likewise, if an individual donor who supports your church or ministry offers to match all contributions made toward a particular project (such as a building fund or the missions budget), recognize the offer for what it is: a timely opportunity to maximize the efficiency of your giving.

A scriptural parallel to leveraged giving may be seen in the parable of the talents, recounted in Matthew 25. Before embarking on a journey, a man summoned his servants and asked them to handle his money. The first servant got five talents (more than $5,000). The next one received two talents ($2,000), while the third man was given just one talent ($1,000).

The master was gone for a long time. When he returned, he found that the fellow who had received five talents had invested the money and doubled his holdings. Likewise, the one with two talents had put the money to work and earned two more. But the man who had been given only one talent had nothing to show for himself. Instead of investing the money, he had nervously buried it in the ground, digging it up only when the master returned.

Branding the fellow lazy, wicked, and worthless, the master ordered the fearful servant tossed out into the darkness. But for the others—the men who had doubled his money—the master had nothing but praise. "Well done, good and faithful servant!" he said to both of them. "You have been faithful with a few things; I will put you in charge of many things. Come and share your master's happiness!"

Like the fearful servant, some churches and ministry workers plod along, unwilling to get in on God's action for fear of where He might lead. They drain their cash resources, with little or nothing to show for it in the end. Leveraged ministries, on the other hand, put the contributions of their members or supporters to work in a way that enhances their overall effectiveness. Like the wise servants, they pursue the highest return, generating the maximum result for every dollar they receive.

When your giving is strategic, passionate, and leveraged, you—like the wise money managers—will be worthy of the Lord's approval: "Well done, good and faithful servant!"

WHERE (Activities)	WHERE (Geographically)				HOW MUCH (1)
	MY CITY	MY STATE	MY COUNTRY	THE WORLD	
EVANGELISM					
DISCIPLESHIP					
POOR					
WIDOWS					
ORPHANS					
TOTAL:	$_____	$_____	$_____	$_____	$_____

Giving Plan

(1) How much to give?

Proportionately	—should:	_____
Planned	—could:	_____
Precommitted	—would:	_____

TOTAL: $_____

For a summary of this section, here are the quick questions I ask myself when considering giving to a ministry:

- Is this ministry strategic?
- Are the ministry efforts leveraged?
- What is this ministry's vision?
- Is the vision God-sized?
- Does it match my heart and passion?

➲Does this ministry show competence? Does it have the organizational capacity to implement its vision (staffing, leadership, financial resources, etc.)?

➲Do the leaders exhibit humility?

The "Giving Plan" chart on page 117 may also help you think through your giving goals. The chart is based on the Great Commission (Matthew 28:19–20) and on the Father's passion for the most important people among us (see Exodus 22:22, Deuteronomy 10:18, and Psalm 68:5). Simply fill in each box with the names of ministries or individuals who come to mind, whom you'd like to give to.

The bottom line is if the Lord is nudging us clearly to give now and we resist because we fear not having enough, then we lack trust in His inspired direction and bountiful provision.

GIVING TO YOUR CHILDREN

So far in this chapter, we have focused on when, why, and how to give to charities. You may have decided to transfer some of your wealth to your children. If you want to include your children in your will but are unsure about their ability to handle money, consider giving them "training" inheritances while you are alive.

When each of their four children reached his or her eighteenth birthday, Sam and Becky gave them a portion of their inheritance. Their goal was to find out how the kids would handle a small amount of money—and, consequently, how they would likely handle more.

Sam and Becky's children may have had good intentions, but being young and relatively inexperienced in financial management, they pretty much wasted the money. But, like the Bible's wayward son who returned to his father, the children learned some valuable lessons from their mistakes. Today, Sam and Becky periodically give their children lump sums of money, and they do a masterful job of handling it wisely.

By demonstrating generosity toward their children, Sam and Becky are sowing and reaping the benefits of "lifetime giving." Sam and Becky are giving their kids "hands on" experience and training in financial management. I have observed that experience is a good teacher; coached experience is a great teacher. In other words, experience coupled with a mentor helping to evaluate and coach through the experience is a great benefit.

Sam and Becky's lifetime gifts have also provided blessings that reach beyond material values. Family vacations that otherwise would not have been possible have become an affordable reality, thanks to Sam and Becky's generosity. Likewise, their gifts have opened the door for a number of their grandchildren to attend private Christian schools—an education that Sam and Becky see as a valuable and practical investment in their family's spiritual, academic, as well as financial future.

I know of many others who have adopted a similar outlook on giving to their children. One couple offered to pay the life insurance premiums for their son-in-law until he could afford to make the payments out of his own salary. Another man gave his children money toward a Roth IRA.

Advantages of Lifetime Giving to Your Children

While practical helps like these obviously involve a financial cost, the benefits they provide can make a significant difference in your children's lives and in their ability to raise a family.

Another advantage of lifetime giving is the effect it can have on reducing your estate taxes. Under the current tax law, you can give away $11,000 per year (adjusted periodically according to inflation index) to as many individuals as you like. In other words, a husband and wife together could give $22,000 a year to each of their four children—thereby reducing the size (and taxability) of their estate by $88,000 each year. By including sons- and daughters-in-law and grandchildren in the distribution plan, the size (and taxability) of the estate could shrink even further. When you are looking for creative ways to minimize estate taxes, taking advantage of the annual gift exclusion can make good economic sense.

One of the best things about giving money to your children (or grandchildren) is the opportunity you get to watch them use it to enrich their lives—an opportunity you would otherwise miss if you waited to distribute your assets through your estate. Per- haps one of your children feels called to be a missionary. Would a financial gift from you help him or her make the vision a real- ity? Likewise, your generosity toward your children, exercised with wisdom, can open doors and alleviate financial burdens when it comes to things like starting a business, buying a first home, or funding your grandchildren's college education.

Unfortunately, lifetime giving also means you have to watch them make mistakes. While you need to be ready to offer finan- cial guidance and advice when your kids ask for it, you must also remember that they can learn from their failures.

There was a young businessman eager to learn from the founder of the company. He went to the wise old man and asked him, "Sir, could you tell me what it takes to become wise like you?"

The wise old businessman paused and said, "Certainly, my son—two words."

The young man then asked, "Please tell me, sir, what are those two words?"

The wise old man answered, "Good decisions."

The young man thought about this and then boldly inquired, "Sir, can you tell me how you learn to make good decisions?"

After thinking for a moment, the wise old businessman said, "Certainly, my son, one word—experience."

Persisting, the young man said, "Please, sir, permit me one more question. How do you get experience?"

The wise old businessman said, "Son, two words—bad decisions."

This story conveys much truth. You learn more from your failures than you do from your successes. I suspect that Peter was a better apostle after his denial of our Lord than he would have been had he not experienced that tremendous failure. He certainly was more teachable and humble afterward.

Failure is a part of life. The issue is not whether children will fail, but how they will respond to failure. The best time for them to fail is while they are young and parents are available to counsel them. (Notice I said "counsel," not "criticize.") Probably the biggest mistake parents make in training children to manage money is not giving them the freedom to fail. Parents either make decisions for them or are so critical of their decisions that children quickly learn not to risk anything on their own.

To be unable to deal with failure in any aspect of life is to be crippled. Christians, of all people, should learn to deal with failure because, in the very act of becoming Christ's followers, we have admitted our failure to live up to God's law. Children must be given an opportunity to fail so that they can learn to cope with failure and not be devastated by it. And you can be comforted to know that even though mistakes were made with the money you provided, many fewer mistakes will probably be made with the larger amounts you may leave at death—if you pass along wisdom and experience while you're living.

Despite the benefits associated with lifetime giving, you may feel financially unable or emotionally unwilling (for whatever reason) to begin passing on your wealth right now. In that case, providing for your heirs by a well-designed wealth transfer plan becomes all the more important.

Guidelines for Giving to Your Children

Overall, I think it is more beneficial to give to your children while you are alive. Regarding current giving to children, Judy and I have practiced the following guidelines. We have tried our best over the years, made some mistakes, and then learned from those mistakes.

➲*Give with no manipulative strings attached*—Gifts should be gifts, not behavioral modification tools. If you are trying to change adult children's behavior by what you do for them financially, that is manipulative. For some parents and grandparents, this poses a challenge. Instead of giving money freely, we may be tempted to want something in return: phone calls, visits during the holidays, a license to "meddle" in our children's marriages, and so on. But those kinds of expectations run contrary to the spirit of generous giving. When you make a gift to your children, be sure it is exactly that: a gift.

➲*Transfer wealth gradually without changing their lifestyle dramatically.* Our youngest son recently moved into a new home in Texas where he is going to law school. We bought him and his wife a new washer and dryer. I think we have done that for all of our kids. If you think about it, a washer and dryer is not going to change their lifestyle one bit. It helped them financially but it didn't change their lifestyle. They are going to use it, probably daily. It is not a luxury item.

Another way my wife and I have helped our adult children is helping pay for their home. Our approach, however, was different than the usual giving of money for a down payment. We waited until our adult children and spouses saved their own money for a down payment. They selected the home they wanted, they chose the mortgage option they wanted, and they settled on a monthly payment they could afford.

Then, we surprised them with a monthly gift to them to help pay down the principal on their mortgage. Our approach doesn't affect their lifestyle, doesn't help them live beyond their means, and doesn't involve surety on our part. We give a certain amount each month to build equity in their home. It's a phenomenal financial help to them because it means they will probably be out of their mortgage debt in ten to fifteen years instead of thirty years.

We enjoy helping them now—when they need the help more—but without keeping them dependent on us. It's our way to take the wealth God has given us and transfer it to them and bless them without changing their lifestyle. We can stop at any time if needed. They would continue making the required monthly mortgage payment, as they do now.

➲ *Respect the need of the husband to provide.* Whether it's our son or son-in-law, we don't want to provide so much that the husband feels he is not needed or has his motivation to work dampened. The hard thing for parents who have some wealth is they could help avoid some of the problems their kids are facing. If our adult children ever became dependent on us—when they could provide for themselves—then we should change the level of financial gifts or help that we give.

➲ *Respect the sanctity of your children's marriages.* We wouldn't want our giving to cause conflict or symbolize taking sides in a disagreement between a husband and wife.

➲ *Respect your children's parental wishes.* Avoid coming between the parents and the grandchildren. Let's say your children respectfully request you to reduce your Christmas giving. Perhaps they feel too many gifts are building more selfish tendencies in their children. Respect their wishes. Don't get into a situation where your desire to give causes problems.

➲*Stay out of the way of God dealing with your children.* It's hard for wealthy parents to watch their kids struggle with problems that could be solved with a check. But it may not always be God's will for you to solve your children's problem with a check. God may have a lesson for them to learn or may want them to seek another solution that He has in mind. The more you have, the more difficult it is to allow your children to be fiscally disciplined and suffer the consequences of their mistakes, because it is easier for you to take away the financial pain.

If you follow these guidelines, giving to your adult children now can be a joy and a blessing to you both.

Giving to your children now also eliminates some of the negative toll inflation can take on your estate. Let's go back to the year 1970. Let's imagine you make a will giving $40,000 to each of your children. This seems like a tremendous sum of money—it is many times the average annual salary of 1970. This sum would easily buy a nice house in the suburbs. But by the time your children receive the money—twenty or thirty years later—the fixed amount of the inheritance may not be that much. To remind you of inflation's effect, think about the financial comments made back in the year 1957:

Comments Made in the Year 1957

"No one can afford to be sick any more; $35 a day in the hospital is too rich for my blood."

"I'll tell you one thing, if things keep going the way they are, it's going to be impossible to buy a week's groceries for $20."

"If they raise the minimum wage to $1, nobody will be able to hire outside help at the store."

"Did you see where some baseball player just signed a contract for $75,000 a year just to play ball?"

"Did you hear the post office is thinking about charging a dime just to mail a letter?"

"When I first started driving, who would have thought gas would someday cost twenty-nine cents a gallon? Guess we'd be better off leaving the car in the garage."

"It's too bad things are so tough nowadays. I see where a few married women are having to work to make ends meet."

"It won't be long before young couples are going to have to hire someone to watch their kids so they can both work."

"There is no sense going to Lincoln or Omaha anymore for a weekend. It costs nearly fifteen dollars a night to stay in a hotel."

"If they think I'll pay fifty cents for a haircut, forget it."

Because of the long-term effects of any inflation, you may consider giving more now to your kids or to your church or other ministries rather than later. If you have defined "How much is enough?" and met that level, then prayerfully consider how your giving could help and bless your heirs and chosen charities now rather than later. After you have made your timing decision, you may need to implement changes in the titling of assets. What does that mean? Read the next chapter to find out.

WHAT IF...

You gave a substantial portion of your wealth to your church in your will after your death. What if God asked you, "Why didn't you join Me in what I was doing twenty years ago at your church and give then?" What would your reasoning be? Would that reasoning hold up to God's scrutiny?

MAY I ASK A FOLLOW-UP QUESTION?

Q. *All of what you have said so far makes sense, but I have not heard or read about some of these concepts before. How does your advice about considering giving to charity rather than children, giving now rather than later, and so on compare to what secular financial experts say?*

A. I am cautious to look for confirmation from secular professionals who have a different worldview. But I can understand—and I'm not offended—why you ask the question. You seek another point of view.

Even though I don't look to the secular world for wisdom, I have observed that truth is ultimately from God. God's truths often find acceptance—although not acknowledged by man. The way He works is mysterious, salvation confounds us, but His principles stand true. Here is a sampling of what other well-known financial authorities have written about some of these topics:

From the best-selling book *Die Broke*, financial planner and attorney Stephen Pollan:

> What good will money do you when you're dead? Creating and maintaining an estate does nothing but damage the person doing the hoarding. It will force you to put the quality of your death before the quality of your life. You'll be forced to choose not to spend something for yourself so your kids can use the money.
>
> There's even evidence that inheritance hurts the recipient. Studies show that the expectation of an inheritance erodes the drive and motivation to work. And what do you think it would do to your soul to have a reason to look forward to the death of a loved one.
>
> Passing on wealth to the next generation might be possible for some, but why do it? It wouldn't be good for you, your child, or society. Now you can use your money while you're alive, doing good for yourself and others.[2]

Warren Buffet, probably the world's most well-known investor, calls inherited wealth "food stamps for the rich." Noted for his financial common sense, he said, "All these people who think that food stamps are debilitating and lead to a cycle of poverty, they're the same ones who go out and want to leave a ton of money to their kids." Buffet later rebutted the rumor that his kids were written out of his will. He said that they've gotten gifts right along, but are not going to live the lives of the super rich.[3]

Dave Ramsey, financial talk-show radio host and best selling author, says,

> The great misunderstanding is that we think we have to hoard to get, when in reality you can only have "more than enough" by releasing ownership spiritually and emotionally, then showing that by giving time and money away.[4]

Jonathan Pond, financial author, TV and radio host, and CPA, says the following on his Website:

> It's certainly understandable to be concerned about passing on your estate in a way that will benefit the children. Stories abound of people who have received fat inheritances, have proceeded to lose all initiative, and have ended up far worse off as an individual or family than they had been prior to the inheritance... substantial inheritance should depend on some demonstration of your heir's ability and inclination to handle money responsibly.

Claude Rosenberg Jr., an investment adviser and author of *Wealth and Wisdom,* found that America and Americans would be much better off if more charitable giving occurred. He proved that people could give not only from their income but also from their net worth:

> What I found was that, on average, most people have been giving far less than they could. My research resulted in a startling conclusion: the charitable donations of the IRS's top income group averaged less than 10 percent of what they could have safely afforded! And a similar pattern existed for other income categories, particularly the high earners.
>
> Consider the impact that grandparents, parents, or aunts and uncles might have on younger generations. Gifts need not be substantial in size to impress the young. What better example for younger people to emulate? What better training for the "do unto others" philosophy that most parents teach? What better example to prove that your actions are consistent with your words?
>
> And there are many more who are acting [giving] now, not waiting for the hereafter. But not enough— not enough recognizing that increased donations representing distinctly affordable portions of either income or corpus are small sacrifices when offset by

the large potential benefits to themselves, to their family and community, and to society.[5]

In addition to the modern secular experts I quoted above, I find the experiences of those with great worldly wealth interesting:

"Inherited wealth is as certain death to ambition as cocaine is to morality."
> Commodore Vanderbilt's grandson, heir to $60 million in 1885

"Fortunes tend to self-destruction by destroying those who inherit them."
> Henry Ford

Q. *Do we disinherit young children? In other words, at what age are children considered adult children?*

A. I do not recommend that people disinherit young children. I would say "young" would be children who remain dependent on your income and support—usually that means children who have not yet graduated from college.

Throughout the book, I have intentionally stated that you should consider carefully the effect of significant inheritances given to "adult children." For young children you still have a responsibility to provide. Also, you don't yet know if special needs may develop as they grow where they may need more assistance than you can estimate now.

JUST DO IT RIGHT!

CLEAN LIVING AND GIVING

Day after day, year after year, Oseola McCarty washed and ironed clothes for white folks in Hattiesburg, Mississippi. Due to the death of an aunt, Miss McCarty had to drop out of the sixth grade to help her mother feed the family. She worked six days a week, often until midnight, for nearly eighty years.

Her highest earnings in a year as a laundress were nine thousand dollars. She tithed regularly to her church, lived frugally, and saved consistently. Living in the same house as her grandmother, she waited to add air conditioning until the early 1990s. She doesn't mind that her black and white television gets only one channel, because she doesn't watch it much. Miss McCarty, in her own words, described herself as a "little old colored woman who walked everywhere."[6]

After arthritis forced her to retire in her late eighties, she shared her wild idea with friends at the local bank where she had always deposited her weekly savings. She wanted to give some of her savings to her church, some to family, but most to the University of Southern Mississippi.

Her ironing clients, her community, and the whole nation was shocked to learn that Miss McCarty had given $150,000 to the University of Southern Mississippi, a school she never attended. All the reporters wanted to know how she did it. Her simple secret: regular saving and compounded interest.

"I'd go to the bank once a month, hold out just enough to cover my expenses, and put the rest into my savings account. Every month, I'd save the same amount and put it away. I was consistent."[7]

By following the Givin' While Livin' Principle, Miss McCarty benefited in several ways. She multiplied her gift with leveraged giving. The ensuing media attention of her sacrifice created much excitement around the nation and inspired many others to give more than $380,000 to her scholarship fund.[8] That's a 253 percent return on her money!

"I try to be a good steward," said Miss McCarty. "I start each day on my knees, saying the Lord's prayer. Then I get busy about my work. I get to cleaning or washing. I find that my life and my work are increasing all the time. I am blessed beyond what I hoped."[9]

Her generosity allowed her to travel the nation in her late eighties and early nineties. She received a doctorate of humane letters from Harvard University, met with the President of the United States, carried the Olympic Torch, and flew to accept awards and interviews with all major networks. If she had waited to give until her death, she would not have been able to inspire others with her simplicity, hard work ethic, and faith.

Bud Kirkpatrick, Director of Public Relations at the University of Southern Mississippi, handled her appointment schedule as she went from relative obscurity to media curiosity. People often asked him how she handled speaking with Barbara Walters and Dan Rather one day and giving speeches to young graduates the next. "She is living out putting God first and trusting that all else will be added to her. She is living out her belief that for every step she takes, God will take two. As she says it, 'I know He will. I know 'cause I have tried that, and it works.'"[10]

Believing that faith and education are essential for success, she sets a high bar for giving sacrificially. As she states simply, "If you want to feel proud of yourself, you have to do things you can be proud of."

Even in the last days before her death, she continues to challenge and inspire, "When I leave this world, I can't take nothing away from here. I'm old and I won't live always—that's why I gave the money to the school and put my affairs in order. My only regret is that I didn't have more to give."[11]

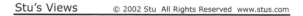

". . . and to my brother-in-law Mike, who always said that health is more valuable than wealth, I leave my treadmill."

YOUR
TITLE
DECISION

6

M y wife recently laughed out loud reading a passage from a
woman's devotional. "The older you get, the tougher it is
to lose weight . . . because by then your body and your fat have
become really good friends."

I think the same can be said about our money or possessions.
After a long time of having control of those assets, it's hard to shed
them. We begin to think that those assets are ours. We take ownership of that business or that stock or that land. We want it safe-
guarded in perpetuity for ourselves and for our line of descendants
because we think it is ours. However, all that is currently within
our control belongs to God.

Common examples of titling changes include the following
situations:

Property titles—A deed evidences ownership of real estate.
Changes to a deed is a titling decision to change the ownership.

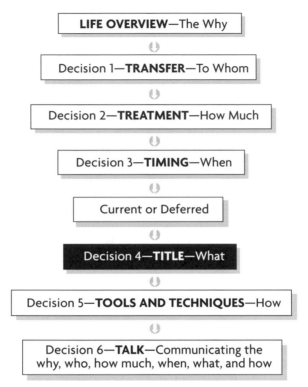

WEALTH TRANSFER
DECISION-MAKING PROCESS

LIFE OVERVIEW—The Why

Decision 1—**TRANSFER**—To Whom

Decision 2—**TREATMENT**—How Much

Decision 3—**TIMING**—When

Current or Deferred

Decision 4—**TITLE**—What

Decision 5—**TOOLS AND TECHNIQUES**—How

Decision 6—**TALK**—Communicating the
why, who, how much, when, what, and how

You may wish to add a child as a joint owner of the family farm or hold rental property as tenants in common with another family member. Some people put their house or vacation property in the name of a spouse or a child to reduce their estate taxes, for asset protection from lawsuits, or to simplify the transfer of wealth. These changes may involve legal risks such as loss of property if your spouse leaves you. That farmland owned jointly with a child may have a lien placed against it if he cannot pay his creditors in a timely fashion.

THE STEWARDSHIP PRINCIPLE God owns it all.

Business succession—Transferring the family business involves titling decisions such as transferring stock, naming directors, or appointing officers of the company. The business owner must decide how much control, income, and future appreciation he wishes to transfer. For example, the founding owner may wish to reduce the control and responsibility but keep an income stream. He could name his daughter as president and let her run the company. He could retain the stock and the annual dividends and remain as a paid consultant. Or, he may wish to transfer the stock to reduce the value of his estate for tax purposes but remain in operational control of the company.

Beneficiary designations—Although neither you nor your beneficiaries will receive these assets while you are still living, another titling decision is choosing your beneficiaries and their respective shares. You transfer your wealth held in 401(k)s, life insurance, individual retirement accounts, and annuities by named beneficiaries.

Trusts—When establishing a trust, you are transferring assets to a separate entity. Whether it is a charitable remainder trust or a life insurance trust, you determine and describe in the trust document what is transferred, when it is transferred, and how it is transferred to the beneficiaries of the trust.

We will talk more about various strategies in chapter 7, "Tools and Techniques Decision," which may involve titling decisions. Remember the sequential nature of the wealth transfer process. Decide to whom and how much and when before starting the titling changes. I recommend obtaining competent legal counsel when contemplating these significant titling changes.

In traditional estate planning, much attention is paid to the titling of assets and attempts to control assets beyond the grave. In the wealth transfer process, I think the Stewardship Principle reminds us of the basic truth: God owns it all.

Chuck Swindoll, author, pastor, former president of Dallas Theological Seminary, and good friend, has heard me speak many times, read my different books, and encouraged me in my ministry. He once told me, "Ron, you really just have one message. All you basically say is that 'God owns it all.'"

Even though Chuck had a bit of teasing in that comment, he's right on the money. I take credit for writing eleven books, but really it's only one book rewritten eleven times! Maybe I'll stop when I feel I've gotten it just right. Understanding God's ownership is foundational to being a good steward. I guess you've noticed that long before this chapter I've said repeatedly, "God owns it all."

WHAT DOES "GOD OWNING IT ALL" HAVE TO DO WITH WEALTH TRANSFER?

After you have decided to whom you will transfer, how much you will transfer to each, and when the transfer will happen, you will actually begin transferring ownership. Unfortunately, many people erroneously focus more of their efforts on the technical aspects of the title decision instead of thinking through the other decisions first. Remember this is a process. You transfer title in order to accomplish the other decisions you have made. The title decision is when you take actual steps to change the deed, transfer the stock, set up the trust, or write the checks.

This is where the rubber meets the road. You may have agreed conceptually with me about givin' while you're livin', but actually writing the check takes faith that this is the right decision. It is much the same as the faith-based response necessary whenever you decide to give to your church or a charity. The business owner may agree with the idea that he needs to set up succession planning for his business, but actually transferring the stock is difficult. Signing the wills to treat your children uniquely takes courage.

One Saturday morning I received an urgent call from a friend about tithing. It's rather unusual to get a financial call on Saturday morning and even more unusual for a tithing question to be urgent. This question actually had more to do about the title decision and God's ownership of family assets.

The grandfather of this family, now deceased, had started a publicly held corporation. He transferred approximately $13 million of the company stock to a trust for the ultimate benefit of his grandchildren and great-grandchildren. The grandchildren, upon reaching various ages, had full control and were able to use trust assets. His grandchildren (the third generation) were now in their sixties and had adult children (fourth generation) of their own.

The caller was one of the third-generation grandchildren. He told me that the trust assets were now worth $36 million. The third-generation children had met with their fourth-generation adult children to inform them they planned to liquidate the trust and tithe from the increase in the assets.

The fourth-generation children protested. They said, "You can't do that. It's our money." So, the third generation asked me what they should do. As I mentioned in chapter 4, sometimes parents have to remember who the steward is and to whom they are accountable. I said that they have the authority under the trust to do as they wish.

Although it was commendable that they talked over their plans with the fourth-generation children, my opinion is that the fourth-generation children didn't grasp the Stewardship Principle. They have the ownership confused. The trust assets are not owned or managed by them, but by the third generation. God owns it all. The third generation, on the other hand, seems to better understand the Stewardship Principle. This is clear by their desire to honor God with a portion of the increase.

As a visual reminder to you, I have provided an ownership "deed" below to help you "sign over" your assets as a spiritual exercise. This deed helps you acknowledge that God owns it and has given you a stewardship responsibility.

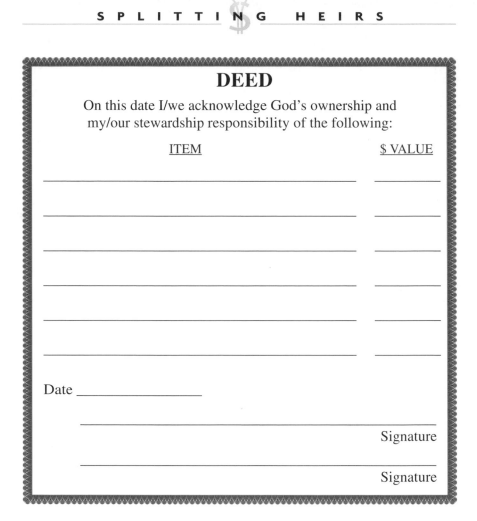

DEED

On this date I/we acknowledge God's ownership and
my/our stewardship responsibility of the following:

ITEM	$ VALUE

Date _____

_____

Signature

_____

Signature

WHERE IN THE BIBLE DOES
IT SAY THAT GOD OWNS IT ALL?

I was once helping a friend, Jim, understand more about applying the Bible to his daily life. When we were discussing the meaning of stewardship, he challenged me, "Show me where in the Bible it says that God owns it all!"

For starters, we looked at Job 41:11, where God tells Job, "Everything under heaven belongs to me."

We read in Psalm 24:1, "The earth is the LORD's, and everything in it, the world, and all who live in it."

Jim was starting to understand, but he wanted more evidence of financial assets, not just the "earth." So, I turned to Haggai 2:8: "'The silver is mine and the gold is mine,' declares the LORD Almighty."

Then, we read 1 Chronicles 29:14. As he watched the Israelites bring forth hundreds of tons of precious metals and gemstones for use in building the temple, King David prayed, "Who am I, and who are my people, that we should be able to give as generously as this? Everything comes from you, and we have given you only what comes from your hand."

Jim was starting to see, but he still had a reservation. He himself earned his money. He worked hard and built up his assets. How could God own it? So, we read in Deuteronomy 8:18, "Remember the LORD your God, for it is he who gives you the ability to produce wealth."

As his final argument, Jim asked, "Is there any support in the New Testament?" I showed him 1 Corinthians 6:19–20, "You are not your own; you were bought at a price." We looked at Jesus' teaching in Matthew 25:14, "[The kingdom of heaven] will be like a man going on a journey, who called his servants and entrusted his property to them."

God owns it all and entrusts it to us for a while. Here's a picture of the role of ownership versus stewardship. As an investment adviser, I managed money for the benefit of clients. The assets I managed did not belong to me or my employees. We had no right to them. They belonged to the clients. My job was to find out what the clients wanted, and then I tried to accomplish those objectives.

At some point, the client wanted to have those assets back. My job would then be done. I would have no claim to retain the assets. The owner had requested them. My stewardship term was over. Think of yourself as God's money manager.

I also like Randy Alcorn's example of us being God's errand boys and delivery girls. We just work here; we don't own the place.

Suppose you have something important you want to get to someone who needs it. You wrap it up and hand it over to the FedEx guy. What would you think if instead of delivering the package, he took it home, opened it, and kept it for himself?

You'd say, "This guy doesn't get it. The packages don't belong to him. He's just the middleman. His job is to get them from me to the person I want him to hand them off to." Just because God puts His money in our hands doesn't mean He intends for it to stay there![1]

WHAT ARE THE IMPLICATIONS OF GOD OWNING IT ALL?

Truly believing that God owns it all has three implications:

1. He can take whatever He wants whenever He wants.
2. Every spending decision is a spiritual decision.
3. Stewardship cannot be faked.

God Can Take What He Wants

If God can take whatever He wants whenever He wants, then hold all resources with an open hand. God puts into your hand whatever He chooses to entrust you with, and He has the right to take out of that hand whatever He desires. When He takes anything out, you, as a steward and manager of His resources, should feel no regrets, because those resources belong to Him. Simply heed the wisdom of these words: "The LORD gave and the LORD has taken away; may the name of the LORD be praised" (Job 1:21).

I have been asked, "How much is enough?" many times; and I believe that it relates to the open-hand principle. When you close your hand and say, "God, You no longer have the right to take Your resources," you have crossed the line from *stewardship* (responsibilities) into *ownership* (rights). I urge you to cross back over, because only God is the true owner.

140

If your heart attitude is one that believes God can take whatever He wants whenever He wants it, your fear of economic uncertainty is removed. If there is an economic collapse of some sort and God destroys our economic system, you can cope, because you recognize that the resources are God's. He is choosing to use them in a different way.

People who hold tightly the ownership rights of their resources have great fear of an economic disaster. It could be a personal disaster and all your personal assets are lost. Or, a national economic collapse may affect everyone in the country. In either case, those who "own" their lives, children, and possessions will be devastated. True stewards may be shaken, but not destroyed, because they know God is at work.

Additionally, believing that God can take whatever He wants whenever He wants will give your decision making its proper perspective. You will make your decisions as a steward. Knowing they are God's resources will give you a long-term perspective and cause you to use spiritual priorities in making financial decisions. The question to ask yourself is this: How does God want me to use these resources? Considering this question will remind you that you are not managing your own resources.

Spending Decisions Are Spiritual Decisions

The second implication of believing that God owns it all is that every spending decision is a spiritual decision. In other words, there is nothing more spiritual about tithing than paying for a vacation. Why? All your resources are God's and all your decisions should be to accomplish His purposes. Now I'm not saying, "Don't tithe." I'm saying that all you have is God's, so all your decisions should be made with His purpose for your life in mind.

For example, the goal may be to build family unity, and a vacation is a way to build that unity. Or, a bouquet of flowers or bottle of perfume may be just the thing to increase romance and closeness between you and your spouse. Another life goal may be to develop a certain talent for God's glory. God gave the gift, and perhaps you will use the money He gave to attend classes, receive instruction, or go to a conference. You can see that money is a tool God uses to achieve the goal of active use of spiritual gifts.

Money is nothing more than one of the resources God uses to accomplish the real goals and objectives of life. For example, one life goal may be security. But the only real security is through a personal relationship with Jesus Christ. Money cannot buy this, and any attempt to use money to buy security will ultimately fail. God will allow it to fail, so you must trust Him for your security both now and for all eternity. God wants you to be secure in Him, not in money. In this case, Christ alone achieves the life goal of security and peace.

Believing that every spending decision is a spiritual decision can have three results. The first one is the freedom that comes from knowing God has an ultimate plan for your life and has given you the financial resources to accomplish that plan. You are freed from the guilt of wondering whether you are spending His resources properly. This is the most exciting result and certainly a positive one.

The other two results are negative because, as human beings, we become legalistic, always wanting a set of rules to live by, and forgetting that we "stand firm . . . [in the] freedom that Christ has set us free" (Galatians 5:1) and that God "richly provides us with everything for our enjoyment" (1 Timothy 6:17).

One of the two results to watch for is guilt. Guilt is most apt to occur when you know that you are spending God's resources on selfish pursuits. You need to realize you have made a presumptuous decision when you use His resources to accomplish *your* purposes and plans rather than *His* purposes and plans. When you step back and once again realize they are God's resources, you can be free to obey what God wants you to do with them.

Such lack of obedience reminds me of a black lab of ours,

Maggie. When she was a year old, Maggie was a seventy-pound bundle of exuberance. Her most endearing characteristic was that she very obviously and desperately wanted to please. When we petted her and gave her attention, she was the most affectionate animal that there could be. However, periodically Maggie would blow it—usually chewing up something that she shouldn't or digging a hole where we did not plan to have one.

When confronted with her disobedience, she cowered low, her ears drooped, and her eyes took on a very sad look. She was unhappy because she knew she made me unhappy. When we pursue our own interests instead of our Lord's, we make Him unhappy. We won't be entirely satisfied again until we are back in favor with our Master, who, in our case, is the Lord Jesus Christ.

The other negative result is rigidity. People who are afraid to make a decision—because of the fear of making a mistake with God's resources—are forever in financial bondage. This bondage occurs regardless of the amount of resources entrusted to them.

At a conference recently, a very shabbily dressed woman approached me. As she talked, I realized that this woman, who appeared to be poverty-stricken, was actually very wealthy. I was shocked as she rattled off large sums of money she had stashed in savings accounts, investments, real estate, and prepayments on a retirement home. Her concern was where to invest money in order to have total security. This woman was so fearful of making a financial mistake that she couldn't experience the freedom of using the resources that God had entrusted to her. Christ has truly made us free, yet she experienced none of His freedom.

Think of the freedom that comes from knowing that God has given you resources to manage and that He has given you guidelines on how to manage them to accomplish the real goals and objectives of life. You are not left alone to make spending decisions. God has given you His Holy Spirit to guide you in wisdom, His Word as a source of truth, and a sound mind to use His resources properly. He has also provided more than enough grace to cover over our inevitable financial blunders, large and small.

Stewardship Can't Be Faked

The third implication of believing that God owns it all is that you can't fake stewardship. Your checkbook tells how you choose to use God's resources. Your checkbook reveals the priorities in your life. It reveals facts such as how you manage your time, what size family you have, where you live, how much debt you have, how much you are allocating to savings and investments, how you dress, and so on.

Every other area, except the financial one, of the Christian life can be faked. A person need only be a Christian for a short time to know how to pray impressively, how to witness with an outline from an evangelism program, where to find a "growing" church, or how to talk with "Christian" words. These can be done without revealing the person's real motive.

However, the checkbook reveals one's actual commitment to the use of God's resources to accomplish God's purposes. I sometimes wonder if, when we get to heaven, all our check registers will have preceded us. If so, would we be reviewing how we used or abused His resources?

HOW CAN WE MAKE
TITLING DECISIONS LESS COMPLICATED?

Implementing titling decisions will have more legal, tax, and financial implications than decisions we've looked at already. Make sure you review these with your advisory team. The same is true with our next decision, The Tools and Techniques Decision.

As you think through the title decision, ask yourself the question, "Am I trying to maintain the control into that third, fourth, and fifth generation?" This happens regularly when setting up trusts where the originator chooses various terms. Even in the best of cases, this extended control can be challenging.

An example I am familiar with is the Maclellan Foundation. It supports more than two hundred ministries and charitable organizations each year. Its purpose is to serve strategic international and national organizations committed to furthering the kingdom of Christ and to select local organizations that foster the spiritual welfare of the Chattanooga, Tennessee, area.

This foundation was set up multiple generations ago. The ultimate disposition of the remaining principal to the family will not occur for another three generations—at least fifty or so years from now! Hugh Maclellan Jr., chief executive officer of the foundation, has done an outstanding job leading the foundation to be true to its original purpose. But the original terms of the foundation call for leaving a significant amount of money to some recipients who may not even be born yet.

This foundation and the trusts preceding it were set up by the creator of the wealth in order to maintain control. So, you have children six or seven generations removed from the creator of the wealth who are going to be the recipients of the wealth. Despite all the good the foundation has done—and the Maclellan Foundation is one of the best foundations I know of—the original creator is exerting control over heirs he's never met! Even in the best of situations, it still is difficult to ensure the original intent of the creator.

After tackling the Title Decision, you are then ready to utilize the tools and techniques to reduce taxes, provide for heirs, and leverage gifts to charity. Read the next chapter for a layman's explanation of these tools and techniques.

WHAT IF...

You were standing before God at the end of your life and He asked, "I chose you to have a better lifestyle and more resources than six billion other people I created. How did you use those resources? How did you leave those resources?"

MAY I ASK A FOLLOW-UP QUESTION?

Q. *Your material makes sense to me, but it appears a bit radical. Almost everyone I have ever known about leaves their money to their family. Do you think the fact that you have been on the board of various not-for-profit charities and spoken at fund-raising conferences has colored your view some?*

A. You are right about the fact that most people simply leave money to their family. Many people do not have wills at all. State law mandates the distribution of the assets for people without wills. This may result in leaving money to family—and not always in the way the person without a will would have wanted.

I believe that Christians are called to be different from most people in the world. I want to challenge people with a thinking process centered on renewing rather than conforming. Romans 12:2 reminds us, "Do not conform any longer to the pattern of this world, but be transformed by the renewing of your mind. Then you will be able to test and approve what God's will is—his good, pleasing and perfect will."

Perhaps part of the reason for the moral decay in our society is that Christians have conformed their wealth to the pattern of this world. We need to change that. Is that radical? I suppose it is if most people don't think through and pray over their wealth transfer plans.

My role as a board member of various organizations has provided me with a unique vantage point in seeing the kingdom needs—as well as the kingdom opportunities— that are around us. I don't think it has caused me to be unfairly biased. It has opened my eyes rather than closed them.

As I have gotten older and helped several generations with managing money, I have observed the waste of significant resources when adult children who already have much amass more wealth. Scripture affirms that God loves cheerful givers. Also, Jesus Himself admitted that His attention was given to the poor and to those who wanted to listen to His Word. I do not apologize for teaching that we can follow His lead when we cheerfully and freely give to causes that build His kingdom, either instead of, or in addition to, our family. That's why I am motivated to share this message with as many people as possible through seminars and this book.

JUST DO IT RIGHT!

HERE'S THE SCOOP ON GIVING FROM THE MAN WHO INVENTED THE SCOOP

At age thirty, R. G. LeTourneau dedicated his life to be God's businessman. By age thirty-one, LeTourneau was five thousand dollars in debt due to an inept partner in a Stockton, California, mechanic repair shop. God didn't appear to have a very successful businessman on His side.

Disengaging himself from the garage, LeTourneau started all over in the earthmoving business with a tractor, and promised to repay his debt to the bank. In 1923, at age thirty-five, Le-Tourneau was granted his first U.S. Patent: #1470853. It was for a scraper. His last patent was granted in 1965 when he was seventy-seven years old. In the forty-two years between these two inventions he was granted 295 more patents and became one of the top inventors of all time.

LeTourneau is credited with the creation of the modern mechanized earthmoving industry. His 297 inventions included the bulldozer, scrapers of all sorts, dredgers, portable cranes, dump wagons, bridge spans, and logging equipment. He invented mobile sea platforms for oil exploration that now dot the seas throughout the world. He introduced the rubber tire into the earthmoving and material handling industry.

When the Allied forces invaded the Normandy beaches on D-Day, they had an impressive display of machines and equipment, much of it built by the energetic American businessman, LeTourneau. His company built 70 percent of the heavy earthmoving equipment used by the Allied forces in World War II. During the height of the war, from 1942 to 1945, his fertile mind pumped out seventy-eight inventions, many of which were instrumental in helping to win the war.

His business efforts—although incredibly successful—never deterred him from what he felt was his reason for existence: to glorify God and spread the Gospel message. For more than thirty years he traveled across the U.S., Canada, and other countries at his own expense sharing his testimony about the satisfaction and joy of a businessman serving Jesus Christ. Each time he spoke he began by saying, "Friends, I'm just a sinner saved by grace. Just a mechanic that the Lord has blessed."

LeTourneau felt it was God's business and he was simply a temporary "partner in business." He was concerned that his dedication to God could be dimmed by his love for his machines, but his commitment to God extended over a period of fifty years. He employed three full-time chaplains and held regular chapel services at his manufacturing plants.

LeTourneau lived for many years on 10 percent of his income and gave away 90 percent to Christian work. He invested millions of dollars in missionary development projects in less-developed countries of Africa and South America. Even in times when his business was in financial jeopardy, he continued giving his sacrificial pledges to Christ's work. "The question" he said, "is not how much of my money I give to God, but rather how much of God's money I keep for myself."

His life's verse was Matthew 6:33: "But seek first his kingdom and his righteousness, and all these things will be given to you as well." LeTourneau proved the promises in this verse. Despite his generous giving during his life and at his death through the LeTourneau Foundation supporting numerous Christian causes, LeTourneau found he couldn't give it away fast enough. In an appropriate earthmoving metaphor, he said, "I shovel it out and God shovels it back—but God has a bigger shovel."[2]

"It was painted by a Tax Accountant shortly after going insane."

Stu's Views

Reading the Will

"To my loyal estate planning attorney, I leave my children a complicated series of trusts that will generate huge legal fees."

YOUR TOOLS
A N D
TECHNIQUES
DECISION

Estate tools and techniques? I realize this may be the chapter where you are likely to flip ahead for the next cartoon. But here you'll learn a simple technique to save more than $500,000 in federal estate taxes. You can also find out how to receive a stream of income the rest of your life while giving to charity. Sound interesting? Then stay with me.

Charitable remainder annuity trusts, foundations, unified estate and gift tax credit, irrevocable trusts—whew! The legal complexity can be overwhelming. I have sometimes shared the frustration Will Rogers had with legal writing. He said,

> The minute you read something and you can't understand it, you can almost be sure that it was drawn up by a lawyer. Then if you give it to another lawyer to read and he don't know just what it means, why then you can be sure it was drawn up by a lawyer. If

it's in a few words and is plain and understandable only one way, it was written by a non-lawyer.

Every time a lawyer writes something, he is not writing for posterity, he is writing so that endless others of his craft can make a living out of trying to figure out what he said, 'course perhaps he hadn't really said anything, that's what makes it hard to explain.

As proof of Will Rogers' comment, I am reminded of a story about a lecture in a law class. The professor asked one of his better students, "Now if you were to give someone an orange, how would you go about it?"

The student replied, "Here's an orange."

The professor was livid. "No! No! You don't seem to understand. Think like a lawyer!"

The student then recited, "OK, I'd tell him, 'I hereby give and convey to you all and singular, my estate and interests, rights, claim, title, and advantages of and in, said orange, together with all its rind, juice, pulp, and seeds, and all rights and advantages with full power to bite, cut, peel, squeeze, and otherwise eat, the same, or give the same away with and without the pulp, juice, rind and seeds, anything herein before or hereinafter or in any deed, or deeds, instruments of whatever nature or kind whatsoever to the contrary in anywise notwithstanding . . ."

Perhaps lawyers have received an unfair portion of jokes. But working within the legal system and trying to address all contingencies can get frustrating. In my opinion, the perception and fear of complex legal and technical matters provide a primary reason that so few people complete the process of will preparation and implementing their wealth transfer plans. They meet with a lawyer or an accountant or adviser. They hear technical terms that overwhelm them. So, they end up letting the latest "draft" of their plans gather dust.

WEALTH TRANSFER
DECISION-MAKING PROCESS

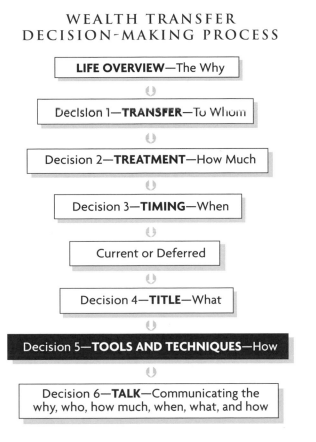

Unfortunately, most people deal with the tools and techniques of wealth transfer too early in the planning process. As I have presented throughout this book, your planning is more competent and complete when you address the decisions such as *to whom* and *how much* before you address the *how*.

Only after you have considered the other decisions in chapters 3–6 should you begin drafting wills, trusts, or other legal instruments. Unfortunately, the tools and techniques, particularly among lawyers and accountants, usually become the focus of planning rather than a tool of planning. The underlying principles of the Tools and Techniques Decision are the following:

THE TOOLS PRINCIPLE⮑Estate planning tools and techniques help you accomplish objectives, but are not *the* objective.

THE TRUST PRINCIPLE⮑Never use a trust because of a lack of trust.

THE K.I.S.S. PRINCIPLE⮑Keep your estate matters as simple as possible.

STRAIGHTFORWARD
PLANNING FUNDAMENTALS—A WILL

Let's start with the basic tool in the wealth transfer process: *your will.* Your will is the foundational cornerstone of an estate plan. It is a written, witnessed document that defines your final wishes and desires regarding many things, including property distribution. A person who dies with a will is called one who dies testate. A person who dies without a will dies intestate, and the laws of intestacy apply.

The laws of intestacy differ from state to state, but in general, if one dies intestate, that person gives the state government the right to determine:

⮑The control of financial resources

⮑The distribution of those resources

⮁The choice of executor

⮑The choice of a guardian for minor children

⮑The ability to waive fiduciary bonds

⮑The right to authorize a business continuation plan

On the other hand, a person who dies with a will retains the following:

⮑The control and the use of assets

⮑The distribution of those assets

➲The bequeathing of specific personal possessions to loved ones

➲The choice of the executor

➲The choice of a guardian for minor children

➲The right to waive fiduciary bonds (such bonds can be expensive)

➲The right to set up various trusts to reduce estate taxes and probate costs

Many Americans don't have a will. Survey after survey reveals that the number of procrastinators ranges from 50–60 percent. An important step for all good stewards is to implement the basic tool of a will. Your good intentions or your prayerful consideration of the wealth transfer process won't get the job done. In many states, the surviving spouse has no say in the matter if there is no will. Your estate becomes subject to the responsibility and function of the court system.

What Do You Put in Your Will?

A will is a document in which you make certain appointments and leave property to certain people or organizations. This is where you describe any specific bequests made after consideration of your Transfer Decision. As part of implementing your Treatment Decision, you would describe specific bequests to individual children and grandchildren. You can even get very specific in a will to specify that the china dishes go to your daughter rather than your daughters-in-law.

To view rather extreme decisions on what to include in a will, see the following excerpts from actual wills compiled from submittals by lawyers in England:

A bit bitter?—Anthony Scott, in his last will and testament wrote: "To my first wife Sue, whom I always promised to mention in my will. Hello Sue!"

155

Some final instructions—The last will and testament of Edith of Walsall included £50,000 to each of her children, Roger, Helen, and Patricia. Their inheritance was not to be spent on "slow horses and fast women and only a very small amount on booze."

Check meaning, not just spelling—One well-meaning will maker gave a legacy to "The Royal Society for the Prevention of Birds." Frank Clifford's will and testament included a legacy to the "Royal Society for the Protection of Cruelty to Animals."

A warm personality?—"I give to Stonyhurst Jesuits the sum of £500 for the purchase of thermal underwear"—Rosaleen's last will and testament, West Yorkshire.

Certainly not a boilerplate provision—"And my ashes shall be handed to Susan H to be scattered in the Chihuahua ring at the Three Counties Show after judging has taken place." Last will and testament of Irene of Swindon.

Hairy conditions for the heirs—In Henry Budd's last will and testament he left £200,000 in 1862 in trust for his two sons on the condition that neither grow a moustache. In another will, Matthias Flemming shared his dislike. He left his employees £10 each in 1869; those with moustaches only got £5, however.

It just doesn't add up—Wills can contain pure gaffs. In his will Philip Hall, professor of pure mathematics, managed to make $2 + 2 + 5 = 10$.

A bit rude?—One man left his employer one shilling to buy a book on manners.

Does Jesus really need it?—Norman Earnest Digweed's will entered the hall of famous wills when he directed that his estate of £26,000 be placed in trust for eighty years for Jesus Christ should he return within that time. Quite a number of people came forward to claim the estate that nevertheless passed to the government after the eighty years was up in 1977.

Canine wills—Miss Amy of Doncaster left £500 to the town's animal shelter requesting it be used to provide dinners at Christmas for dogs in their care.

Feline wills—One cat-loving lady left her whole house to be used to provide for her cat. The lady's funeral was held on a clear spring day, and her cat was sunning itself lazily on the drive outside when sadly it was run over by the hearse.

Wills can be a laugh, but worse than a laughable will is the fact that many people die with no will or wealth transfer plan. Often the government benefits while their families, friends, and charities lose. Don't be one of the millions of people who die each year without a will.

Many people erroneously believe that if they have a small estate, everything will go to the surviving spouse. Therefore, they see no reason to have a will. On the contrary, your assets may not all go to the spouse; they may be allocated among the children and the spouse. The spouse may not have much say over how the children's portion is managed, either.

You cannot simply tell your family members what you want done with your property after your death. Oral expressions made during your lifetime have no legal standing when you are dead. I urge you to have a will that is executed (signed and witnessed properly) and valid under your particular state's laws.

Not Just a Final Testament but a Final Testimony

In his book *A Life Well Spent,* my colleague Russ Crosson recommends including a personal testimony in your will. I agree. As Russ says, your testimony is an explanation of your faith and philosophy, which will be your final statement—your "parting words," if you will—to your posterity when your will is read after your death. There is no better place to take a clear stand about your faith and your commitment to a godly posterity.

Besides a testimony to your family, keep in mind that many strangers may read your will, such as attorneys, accountants, clerks filing it in court, officers of charitable organizations receiving bequests, and others viewing it at a public records office. Consider including a testimony along these lines to introduce your will:

> I, _____ (your name) of
> _____ (city, state, country), being of
> sound mind and with full confidence and trust in my Lord
> and Savior, Jesus Christ, and His death on the cross and shed
> blood as an atonement for my sins, and knowing that by faith
> in His sacrifice on the cross for me I have eternal life, and
> being desirous of directing what disposition shall be made
> of the material wealth and earthly possessions with which God
> in His infinite knowledge, wisdom, and mercy has seen fit to
> bless and bestow upon me, do therefore make, publish, and
> declare this to be my last Will and Testament.

Naming Names . . .

An important appointment made in your will can improve your peace of mind. In your will, you will appoint an *executor* and a *guardian* (if your children are minors). The *executor* is responsible for assuming the property belonging to the estate, safeguarding and ensuring the estate property during the period of estate settlement, and temporarily managing the estate while the estate is being settled. The person you designate will be involved in paying the estate taxes and expenses, accounting for the estate administration, and making distribution of the net estate to the heirs. The duties of the executor can be very time-consuming, frustrating, and complicated. To a surviving spouse, it can be overwhelming. If you have more than one adult child, choosing one of them as executor could possibly sow seeds for mistrust and resentment among the children. You may choose in your will a qualified individual (such as an accountant or a lawyer or trusted friend) or corporate trust company (such as a bank) to assist or fulfill all these duties.

The *guardian* is someone you would trust to take over the care and upbringing of your minor children if something were to happen to each of you. Consider the financial situation of the potential guardian; his or her health, age, and spiritual maturity; and the compatibility of that person's values with yours. Include in your will alternate choices of guardians. Don't forget to obtain permission from any named guardians and executors. Without a will, if both parents should die in a common accident, the court will determine the guardian(s) of minor-aged children.

WHERE THERE'S A WILL—
SOME QUESTIONS AND ANSWERS

Does Having a Will Distribute All My Wealth According to My Wishes?

No, not necessarily. Some assets pass outside of your will. *Check your beneficiary designations on 401(k)s, IRAs, annuities, and life insurance.*

You may have taken great pains to word your will, name heirs, and get your will completed. If so, I commend you. But don't miss something that may not appear obvious—naming beneficiaries. The total value of your IRAs, 401(k)s, and life insurance will pass directly to the named beneficiaries *regardless* of what is in your will. For many people, the majority of their wealth may be passed directly to beneficiaries.

Missing the opportunity to align your beneficiary designations with your wealth transfer plans reminds me of a Sherlock Holmes joke. Sherlock Holmes and Dr. Watson were on a camping trip. After a good dinner by the campfire, they retired for the night. Several hours later, Holmes awoke and nudged his faithful friend.

"Watson, wake up and tell me what you see."

"I see millions of stars, Holmes."

"And what do you deduce from that, Watson?"

Watson pondered the question and finally said, "Well, astronomically it tells me that there are billions of galaxies and planets. Astrologically, I observe that Saturn is in Leo. Horologically, I deduce that the time is approximately a quarter past three. Meteorologically, I suspect that we will have a beautiful day tomorrow. Theologically, I can see that God is all-powerful, and that we are a small part of the universe."

Feeling rather pleased with his thorough observations, Watson then asked Holmes, "What does it tell you, Sherlock?"

Holmes rolled his eyes, "Watson, you idiot! It tells me that someone has stolen our tent!"

By not updating your beneficiary designations regularly, you could make the mistake Watson made—going to great lengths to cover everything but missing the obvious.

Will I Have to Pay Estate Taxes or the So-Called "Death" Taxes?

Since 1916, the federal government of the United States has levied taxes on estates. The original and continuing official rationale is that the estate tax prevents the concentration of wealth. In reality, the estate tax is another means of raising revenue for a government eager to spend it. If its aim were to prevent concentration of wealth, then the tax would be based on what each heir receives rather than what the deceased person owned. The estate tax is the same on the deceased person's wealth whether one person receives it or thirty people receive it.

In a technical sense, you do not pay the estate tax. You have to die before it applies. Your estate will pay the tax. So, your heirs would receive fewer assets after estate taxes are paid. Here's the equation: Your total assets owned at death minus any estate taxes owed equals the amount available for your heirs. The irritating aspect of the estate tax is that much of your wealth has already been taxed for income taxes when you earned it. Let's say that you worked as an employee for forty years and diligently saved and invested your earnings. You paid income tax throughout your working life on the wages earned and the interest and dividends earned. If you did a great job of saving and investing to build an account of $2 million, then your estate may have to pay estate taxes too—at very high rates (minimum of 18 percent rising very quickly to a top rate of 48 percent).

Notice in the last sentence that I said your estate "may" have to pay estate taxes. Despite the bad news that wealth may be taxed twice, the good news is that everyone receives a standard credit from estate and gift taxes. (I have added gift taxes because the estate and gift taxes are related to each other. You can't escape estate taxes by giving away everything—because gift taxes would likely then apply.) This standard credit is technically called the *unified credit*. It is an estate and gift tax credit allowed by law to offset any estate or gift tax due on any transfers of property that are taxed. The amount of the unified credit effective for 2004 is $555,800. This credit will offset the tax on an estate totaling $1.5 million. So, you can give away or transfer to individuals up to $1.5 million without triggering estate or gift taxes. Accountants and lawyers refer to this amount as the technical term "exemption equivalent," but I will refer to it as the Lifetime Exemption.

For many years, the Lifetime Exemption was $600,000. In response to their constituents, Congress raised the Lifetime Exemption effective in 2000. The Tax Act of 2001 implemented a gradual phase-in increasing it to $3.5 million in the year 2009. Effective for 2010, the estate tax is entirely repealed. Then, as a strange result of political compromise, the estate tax comes back! And it reverts back to the rates in place during 2002 when the Lifetime Exemption was $1 million. So, now you must choose a tax-effective year to die!

I mention the future planned chaos in the federal estate tax code to point out that these rates and approaches to taxation are in constant change. The concepts and ideas presented in this chapter will likely continue to apply despite changes in the estate and gift tax rates and in the Lifetime Exemption. Congress and the president may radically change the nature and amount of the estate tax rules. Recognizing this reality of change should result in your periodic review of your wealth transfer plans with a competent tax professional. I will use a Lifetime Exemption amount of $1.5 million for illustrative purpose in the remainder of this chapter.

Let me sum up the basic aspects of estate taxes we have learned so far with the example of Widow Smith. Widow Smith completed the Quantifying Your Wealth to Transfer worksheet on pages 42–43. Her estimated assets available at her death total $1.3 million. This includes her house, CDs, investments, IRA, and the life insurance amount her beneficiaries will receive. She made no significant gifts to individuals during her lifetime. Widow Smith's estate will owe zero in estate taxes. Her heirs will not even have to file an estate tax return because the total value of her estate is less than the Lifetime Exemption of $1.5 million. You may already feel relieved if your estate value is well under the current Lifetime Exemption.

How Do Estate Taxes Apply if I Leave Everything to My Spouse?

You can leave an unlimited amount of property to your spouse and your estate will not have to pay any estate taxes. This sounds too good to be true, right? It is true, but there may be a trap. Let me explain further and use the concept of "Lifetime Exemption" we discussed in the last section.

A *marital deduction* means property that one spouse can transfer to the living spouse at his or her death without paying an estate tax. The amount is unlimited. This can enable a person to avoid all estate tax at the death of the first spouse. The same idea applies to lifetime gifts. The *marital gift exclusion* allows one spouse to transfer an unlimited amount to the other spouse before death without paying a gift transfer tax.

As an illustration, let's say that Tom dies and leaves his land holdings worth $5 million to his wife, Gerri. Because of the unlimited marital deduction, no estate tax is due upon his death. Sounds good so far, but the trap comes at Gerri's death. Let's further assume that she suffered from extreme grief from Tom's death and died the following month. Her estate will be taxed. How much of Gerri's estate will be taxable? The taxable portion will be $3.5 million ($5 million less her Lifetime Exemption of $1.5 million).

Remember that the Lifetime Exemption applies to *each* person. Tom has $1.5 million and Gerri has $1.5 million that they can exempt from estate taxes. The Lifetime Exemption dies with you. So, Tom did not benefit from his $1.5 million Lifetime Exemption. He transferred everything to his wife, Gerri. No estate taxes were owed at Tom's death because of the unlimited marital deduction. He didn't use the Lifetime Exemption, it died with him, and his family lost the benefit of it. We will look at tools and techniques to preserve the value of the Lifetime Exemption in a following section.

How Do Gifts Affect Estate Taxes?

The estate and gift tax laws state that any gifts made during the last three years of a person's life must be counted in the deceased person's estate. Gifts are still considered, on paper at least, as part of a person's estate and are taxed if given within the last three years of life. These laws then effectively limit "deathbed" gifts or signing over of deeds to reduce estate taxes.

Another important concept with gifts is the *annual gift exclusion*. The annual gift exclusion is simply the dollar amount of an asset that can be transferred every year from any person to any other person or persons free from any gift taxes and without using up any of your unified credit. As of 2004, the annual gift exclusion amount is $11,000. For many years the amount was $10,000 per person.

Remember that the estate and gift taxation system works together; it is unified. If John makes a single gift of $500,000 in stock to his son, then gift tax is due (because this is more than the $11,000 annual exclusion amount). John can pay the gift tax in the year the gift was made. Or, John may choose to not pay gift tax now, but he will use up $489,000 of his Lifetime Exemption for estate taxes. If John's total estate is expected to be less than $1.5 million, he can safely use up some of his unified credit because his estate will not owe estate taxes.

Is It True That Life Insurance Proceeds Count as Part of My Estate and May Be Subject to Estate Taxes?

Yes—if you own the policy. I understand that it may seem odd that your estate will be taxed on something you never received. Life insurance proceeds made payable to your beneficiaries will be added back to your estate for purposes of the estate taxes.

Let's use an extreme example to illustrate this. Barbara had $100,000 in a CD and a house worth $150,000. Therefore, her assets owned before death total $250,000. She owned a life insurance policy for $2 million with her only daughter named as beneficiary. Upon Barbara's death, her estate will be valued at $2,250,000. The taxable portion will be $750,000 (the total estate value less the Lifetime Exemption).

Some people wisely use life insurance to provide liquidity at the time of death, to provide for survivors, and perhaps to pay estate taxes. Others may not have a need for life insurance. Keep in mind that unless the ownership is properly structured, the life insurance will be added back to your estate's value when computing the estate tax due. (Stay tuned for a tip to structure this properly.)

TURNING THESE BASICS INTO FIVE WAYS TO SAVE A HALF MILLION IN TAXES

Now that you have some facts, let's see how they might apply.

Although the estate tax seems onerous, the good news is that it is the easiest tax to legally avoid. Minimizing your tax is a valid goal of a good steward, but it is not the most important aim. Remember the Tools Principle: Estate planning tools and techniques help you accomplish objectives, but are not *the* objective. If your objective is to give generously to charity and to your adult children, then minimizing taxes supports your objective. Less to the government means more to charity and to your children.

After you complete the wealth transfer decisions presented so far, if the value of your estimated estate is likely to be more than $1.5 million, then consider the following ideas to save literally hundreds of thousands of dollars in estate taxes. These are simple steps. They are not the most advanced steps, but the K.I.S.S. Principle (from the saying "keep it simple, stupid") reminds us that we do not need to be more complex than necessary to reach our objectives and to minimize taxes.

1. Maximize the Lifetime Exemption by retitling property between the spouses and passing some property to eventual heirs upon the death of the first spouse.

Because each person gets a Lifetime Exemption ($1.5 million in 2004), use that exemption. Instead of transferring all your assets to your spouse, transfer an amount equal to the Lifetime Exemption to your adult children or some organization upon your death. The benefit: Your eventual heirs will get assets earlier and there is less property in the estate of the second spouse. Less property means less tax.

Let's revisit the example of Tom and Gerri that I previously used when explaining the marital deduction. Tom had a total of $5 million in land holdings. These properties were held jointly with his wife. If Tom had a few properties that totaled $1.5 million in value, he could change the title so he owned it individually. In his will, Tom could have these properties he owns individually transferred to his children. Then, the $1.5 million in assets transferred would be offset by the $1.5 Lifetime Exemption resulting in no estate taxes. After his wife, Gerri, died, her estate of $3.5 million would be able to deduct the Lifetime Exemption of $1.5 million. Only $2 million of her estate would be taxed. Thus, each spouse was able to use the Lifetime Exemption. Voila! Tax savings of more than $500,000.

While this idea may work in some cases, there may be practical problems. What if the assets are not easily divisible into a portion equaling the Lifetime Exemption? What if the surviving spouse needs the income from the assets to live on? These practical challenges lead to the second idea—another way to maximize the Lifetime Exemption . . .

2. *Maximize the Lifetime Exemption by using a marital (or A-B) trust.*

The most common type of will, and the simplest, is the "I Love You" or "Simple" will. This type of will simply states that the first spouse to die leaves everything to the surviving spouse using the unlimited marital deduction. This means that if all assets are left to your spouse, no estate tax is due upon the death of the first spouse. This will is satisfactory (from a tax minimization viewpoint) for an estate that is under $1.5 million. As I have already pointed out, substantial taxes could result at the surviving spouse's death if the estate is over $1.5 million. To avoid this large, potential tax problem at the death of the survivor, the second common type of will is used.

The second type of will is the A-B will. This type of will sets up one or two trusts. The objective is to keep a portion of the assets in the estate of the first spouse to die to utilize the Lifetime Exemption. (Sometimes the resulting trust is called a bypass trust because the principal bypasses the spouse.)

For example, this type of will, instead of leaving everything to the spouse, will say something like "I leave everything to my spouse [outright or in trust] except the maximum amount I can keep in my estate and not be subject to estate tax [which, of course, could be as much as $1.5 million]. The amount kept in my estate will go into trust for the benefit of my spouse." A trust is simply a separate taxable entity that is set up during life or through a will to enable an individual to accomplish different desired planning objectives.

If the first amount is left outright, you will have one trust. If it is left in trust, you end up with two trusts. Refer to the figure on the following page. (The legalese will be much different from what I have stated, but in essence that is what happens.)

A-B WILL EXAMPLE WITH TWO TRUSTS

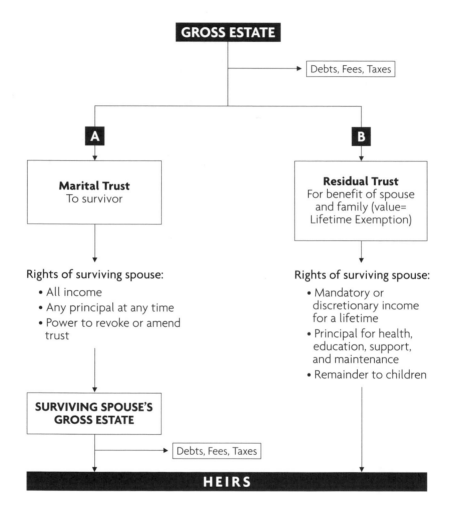

The terms of the trust that will hold the assets left in the decedent's estate (the first to die) are then written in such a way that the survivor has "virtual" ownership of the assets in the trust. In other words, he or she can get income and principal from the trust as needed. Another benefit of the trust is that it provides the surviving spouse with the assistance of a trustee in managing and investing the assets.

By the way, the *trustee* is responsible for managing the estate left in trust in accordance with the terms of your will. The trustee could be a corporation, such as a bank, or an individual. I typically recommend having an individual trustee because he or she is likely to be more responsive to the needs of the surviving spouse. This does not negate the fact that in many specific cases a bank trustee is preferred. Professional counsel should be sought in making this trustee selection.

The executor and the trustee can be one and the same. The trustee does not necessarily need to be knowledgeable in financial affairs, although that may help. Trustees usually seek outside expert financial advice from someone in the business (trust department, financial planning firm). The key concerns in appointing both the executor and trustee are the following: Are they trustworthy? Will they be sensitive to the needs of your family? Do they have integrity? Do they have wisdom not to be taken advantage of?

The A-B will and marital trusts are a common technique. Although there is a bit of setup work, you can save well over $500,000 in taxes, your spouse still has the benefits of the income, and assets are safeguarded for the eventual heirs.

3. *Begin giving gifts now to individual heirs to take advantage of the annual gift exclusion.*

As I mentioned in the Timing Decision (chapter 5), you may decide that giving to your adult children currently—rather than after your death—benefits them more. If your estate may be subject to taxes, an added reason to give now is the reduction in your estate and, consequently, the reduction in taxes. Every $11,000 gift saves between $4,000 and $5,000 in taxes. Everyone wins—except the IRS.

The exclusion provides for an attractive way to remove assets from one's estate with no legal fees or complication—a great example of the K.I.S.S. Principle. For an illustration of how this can work in fairly large numbers, let's assume that Jay and Carol have plenty of income to live on through pensions and rental income and they plan on transferring their wealth to their children and grandchildren. They have three children, all of whom are married and have two children. The three children plus three spouses plus six more children make a total of twelve family members. Because the husband and wife can each give $11,000 to each family member, potentially each can give $132,000 ($11,000 x 12). Combined, they can give $264,000 every year to their family— $11,000 from each parent to each child, spouse, and grandchild.

Remember that the three-year time limit must be satisfied for gifts to be excluded from your estate. This technique—an application of the Givin' While Livin' Principle—can save a very significant amount of estate taxes. I can't estimate specifically how much it will save for you, because it depends on how long you live, how long you give, and the number of people you give to. You can leverage this idea even further. . . .

4. *Give away assets that will likely appreciate rapidly in value to reduce the future potential value of your estate.*

This idea is essentially a turbo-charged version of item #3 above. Instead of giving cash each year, you could give shares of stock or land that may increase in value in the future. By doing so, you eliminate future growth of your estate and limit estate taxes.

Let's say that in 1988 you bought 600 shares of a growing software company for $30,000. The stock began to increase and you believed that one day this relatively small software company could dominate the technology world. You gave 150 shares to each of your four children at Christmas 1988. Based on the value of the stock at Christmas, you gave each of them a gift that was valued at $9,000—less than the annual gift exclusion. Therefore, no taxation resulted at the time of the gift and no usage of your unified credit occurred.

Your children held on to the shares of that company, which later did dominate the technology world. If you had held on to the stock within your estate, then all of the increase would be subject to estate tax. But giving away the stock before it appreciated allowed you to leverage your tax-free wealth transfer. The potential tax savings could range from a few thousand to theoretically a few million dollars given the right circumstances.

If you own assets that have already appreciated substantially, then it may be wiser to hold these or use a more advanced technique described later in this chapter. My standard advice is to work with a certified public accountant and/or your lawyer to understand the potential income tax and estate tax impact of giving business or investment property.

5. *Use an irrevocable life insurance trust (ILIT) to exclude life insurance proceeds from your estate.*

With a wee bit of legal work, setting up an ILIT can save a very significant amount of estate taxes. In simplified terms, here's how this idea works.

The ILIT, that is the trust, owns the insurance policy. You are the insured. When you set up the ILIT, you name the beneficiaries of it. You also name the trustee of the ILIT. You pay the premiums each year; this action is considered a contribution to the trust. The trustee makes sure the premiums are paid, receives notices, notifies the insurance company upon your death, and basically has the power to act on behalf of the trust.

In essence, you have given up ownership of the policy in exchange for getting proceeds to beneficiaries of your choice. Because life insurance proceeds are not taxable for income taxes, your beneficiaries receive the full value of the insurance death benefit. No estate taxes are subtracted and no income taxes are subtracted.

Just one of these ideas is well worth the price of this book! Perhaps you may apply one or more of them if they make sense for your facts and circumstances. Once again, check with your professional legal and tax advisers to ensure compliance with current tax provisions and avoid any other problems or challenges with your situation.

MORE ADVANCED AND
CREATIVE TOOLS AND TECHNIQUES

If you have more significant wealth or special needs, then a whole alphabet soup of creative tools and techniques exist. If you hear the acronyms CRAT, CRUT, CLAT, GRIT, GRAT, and GRUT, they can make you feel Crummey (sorry for such a crummy pun that only a tax lawyer specializing in Crummey trusts could appreciate!).

Patrick is the third generation of his family to farm 250 acres located near a major metropolitan area. When Patrick's grandfather originally bought the land, it was way out in the country, an hour's drive over gravel roads and two-lane highways to reach the major city. As the city grew and its suburbs expanded, Patrick's farm was surrounded by affluent houses and interstate highways.

Patrick resisted the many offers over the years for his land. Farming was all he had known and he held the hope that his sons might want to join him. Eventually, Patrick saw the land was worth far more than he could ever earn farming. His sons graduated from college, obtained advanced degrees, and went off to high-paying jobs in other large cities. A shopping mall developer recently called Patrick with an offer for an eye-popping $25 million for his land.

As he considered whether or not to sell the land, Patrick reviewed his wealth transfer plans with his financial and legal advisers. Patrick and his wife, now in their seventies, needed regular income to support them. They were very interested in funding mission work through their church and other ministries. Their sons were in sound financial condition. Patrick's tax basis for income tax purposes in the land was only $1 million. If he sold the land and received the proceeds, then he would have to pay more than $5 million in income taxes. Then, upon their deaths, their estate would have to pay even more in estate taxes if the remaining proceeds remained in their bank accounts or investment accounts. What could they do?

Their advisers recommended a charitable remainder trust (CRT). The concept of a CRT is that Patrick and his wife donate the property to a trust, the trust sells the property, and the trust invests the proceeds. Patrick and his wife receive an annual income stream from the trust. After their deaths, the remaining principal in the trust is transferred to charity. Hence the name—charitable remainder trust.

What are the benefits of a CRT? First, income tax is avoided. Because Patrick does not sell the property and receive all the proceeds, he does not have to pay income taxes. Not only does Patrick avoid income taxes, he gets a charitable deduction (for a small portion—computed according to IRS formula) for his future gift to charity. Another advantage is that the land and its proceeds are excluded from their estate. The CRT results in millions of dollars of tax savings for Patrick. Patrick and his wife can name one or more charitable beneficiaries, and they have the power to change beneficiaries if desired.

While living, Patrick and his wife will continue to receive a regular income stream. They may choose the method of receiving that income. If they chose to receive a fixed dollar amount, then it is called a charitable remainder annuity trust (CRAT). If they chose to receive 5 percent (the required minimum), then they would receive $1,250,000 per year—far more than they earned farming! The other choice is to receive a fixed percentage. The fixed percentage, called a unitrust (CRUT), is applied against the trust assets. If the investments in the trust increased in value, then the annual payout would increase in value. If the investments decreased, then the annual payout would decrease.

I used Patrick's situation as an example of using a more advanced technique to achieve his objectives. Using a CRAT or CRUT is not always the perfect solution. Remember the Tools Principle—it depends on your objectives. The CRAT or CRUT costs additional legal fees, trust administration fees, investment fees, and tax preparation fees. Another potential concern is that the charities do not benefit until later. If you consider the Timing Decision and prayerfully conclude that the Lord is leading you to give now, then a "remainder" trust would not be the appropriate tool to reach your objectives.

Another tool to benefit a charity now and your family later is a charitable lead trust. This flip-flops the CRT. With a charitable lead trust (CLT), you transfer assets to a trust and the charity receives the income now. Your heirs will receive the remaining principal later upon your death. The CLT works well if you have other sources of income now, the charity needs the income now, and you desire assets to revert back to your heirs.

Many other advanced tools and techniques exist that are beyond the scope—and perhaps beyond the attention span of readers—of this book. Let me finish this section by recommending the use of a lawyer specializing in estates and trusts. Involve your certified public accountant and financial adviser. If you are charitably inclined, keep in mind that many charitable organizations have a development and planning office that can assist you. Many of them provide will and estate planning services at no charge. Although they do desire of course that you include them in your wealth transfer plans, they are competent and helpful. Many provide annuity payments to you in exchange for your significant contributions.

Using these various tools wisely, you can achieve, and perhaps leverage, a wise wealth transfer. For some reason, though, many refuse to even consider such tools. So much more could be done for our churches, our communities, and our own families by using valid, legal, and effective tools and techniques. Why do so many refuse to use the available tools and techniques—from a simple will to a more advanced trust? Perhaps they are misled by one or more myths.

MYTHS FOR NOT USING TOOLS AND TECHNIQUES

"My estate is too small."

An estate may be too small to have estate taxes due on it, but there is more to an estate plan than just the tax aspects. Appointing a guardian to care for any children is far too important a matter to be left to a total stranger. In addition, a relatively simple will can avoid many of the administrative costs associated with death.

When considering the size of an estate, many people forget that life insurance can add significantly to an estate size and may cause not only tax problems, but other problems as well.

One other reason for planning the estate rather than leaving it for the state court system to handle is that any particular personal effects you want to go to specific relatives or friends must be designated in a will. Otherwise, your intentions mean nothing, and the law of the land will determine who gets what.

"It's too expensive."

Many people are "penny-wise and pound-foolish" and think that a will and other actions necessary for proper estate planning are too expensive. First of all, that thought may be an assumption and not a fact. You may easily save ten to one hundred times the cost of will preparation in taxes! My recommendation is to get an estimate or several estimates from those qualified to prepare the documents. Also, probably no price is too great to pay for making it easier on friends and family who have never had to experience life without you.

"I don't have enough time."

The underlying reason for this myth is probably a fear of death. Many people superstitiously believe that as long as they don't prepare a will, they won't die. Also, many just avoid talking about death. It is a very uncomfortable topic of discussion for them. Again, with certainty, everyone will die, and for the Christian to be superstitious about his or her death is to have a poor understanding of the promises God has made in the Bible.

"I'm not certain about what I want to do."

Because estate planning can be a very complex and certainly unfamiliar topic, many do not know how to go about setting those objectives. This is a legitimate concern. However, God promises to provide us the wisdom that we need (see James 1:5). When we are planning for the future, we certainly need God's wisdom.

Also, your wealth transfer plans should be written in sand, not concrete. The design should always be flexible since our needs, desires, and circumstances change over time. So, go on now and make your will. Get your tools and techniques in place to accomplish your objectives. Then, talk about it with your family. See why in the next chapter.

WHAT IF...

You and your spouse died in a car wreck. Does anyone else know where your will and important documents are kept? Does your family know who the trusted advisers are to help them if both of you died?

MAY I ASK A FOLLOW-UP QUESTION?

Q. *I am planning on using a trust upon my death for my wife. My reasoning is that she doesn't like handling money. Also, I wouldn't want some scoundrel of a man to take advantage of her and live off all I have earned. But your Trust Principle made me think that my approach may be off. Does my thinking violate the Trust Principle?*

A. No, I don't think your concern violates the Trust Principle. It *validates* the Trust Principle. You are not using a trust for the wrong reasons. It appears that your motives are to preserve assets for your wife and to provide for her. You, knowing your wife best, seem to think she might be susceptible to losing those assets in some way.

I knew of a situation where a widow was left with a million dollars. She moved to the warm climate of Arizona. She later married the golf pro at the senior community where she lived. He persuaded her to change the title of her assets so they were in his name only. You can see what's coming—he later left her. Of course, he didn't leave the assets. He took all of her wealth. She could do nothing legally to recover them. If her first husband had set up a trust with some protective provisions, then the unfortunate situation of this widow may not have occurred.

Trusts can be useful. My wife's grandfather died and left about $100,000 with a trust department at a local bank for them to invest the money and provide for his wife's needs. In thirty-seven years—she lived to be over 100—she never ran out of money. In fact, when she died her estate was worth over $1 million. The deceased husband's wisdom provided adequately for her, and the wise investment resulted in a large inheritance for the heirs and charities.

Too often, however, people use the tool of the trust because the recipient has very little wisdom to handle money. Rather than only transfer wealth, remember the Wisdom Principle in chapter 3—transfer wisdom first. Don't use the vehicle of a trust to transfer wealth to a participant who is untrustworthy or lacks wisdom. Teach wisdom and develop trustworthy character. If neither is possible, then why would you transfer wealth and choose unwise heirs as the next steward?

JUST DO IT RIGHT!

A G I A N T A M O N G M E N

He's used to ducking through doorways, signing autographs for young fans, and winning basketball games. At 7'1", David Robinson has enjoyed spectacular success as a professional basketball player for the San Antonio Spurs. He was named Most Valuable Player in 1995, won the Sportsmanship Award in 2001, led his team to two championships, and was the only male basketball player to represent the United States on three separate U.S. Olympic teams.

David was a standout even before his professional basketball career began. Despite having the frame of a basketball player, he played classical piano and made a college entrance test score in the 99th percentile. David attended and graduated from the U.S. Naval Academy with a degree in mathematics. He honored his commitment to serve two years in the Navy before joining the pros.

If you talk with David, he would prefer to talk about his relationship with Jesus Christ rather than basketball or his accomplishments. "He'll talk your ear off about that," says Glenn Rogers, a sportswriter who covers basketball for the *San Antonio Express-News,* Robinson's hometown newspaper. "He's found his faith. That's what he goes by."[1]

In an era of ego-driven athletes, David's desire is to follow what God has called him to do with his fame and fortune. David used a "tool" called a foundation to direct his generous giving. The David Robinson Foundation is a Christian organization whose mission is to support programs that address the physical and spiritual needs of the family.

In what is believed to be the largest donation by a professional player, Robinson pledged $9 million toward the establishment of Carver Academy, a private Christian school. In addition to his money, Robinson used his influence to serve as chairman and help raise additional money. His faith-based foundation has provided special seats (in a section called "Mr. Robinson's Neighborhood") he reserves for underprivileged families during Spurs home games; supports faith-based values programs for public school children; and helps lower-income parents pay for college.

What motivated David and his wife, Valerie, to give so generously of their time and resources? "Jesus Christ, as my example, reached out to people in His community who had needs. I want to show my love of God."[2]

Robinson acknowledges that basketball can have some drawbacks. "For one, our salaries are ridiculous compared to more valuable services in society." But, he feels that basketball has given him a platform from which to shine his light. "I can go

into a high school and talk about Jesus. What an incredible opportunity. There are a lot of positive things I see as the reason
God placed me there."[3]

His foundation's motto, emblazoned on its logo, is appropriate for someone standing tall: *"You are the light of the world. A
city on a hill cannot be hidden"* (Matthew 5:14).

"I'm not convinced that's the best strategy.
Then again, I wasn't listening."

*"Everything I have, son, I have because your grandfather left
it to me. I see now that that was a bad thing."*

YOUR TALK DECISION

Is it easier to share your wealth transfer plans with your children around the coffee table or from your coffin? Who can better discuss your motivations, hopes, desires, and blessings with your family: you, or your lawyer reading your will?

If you have diligently worked through the wealth transfer process I've presented, but failed to complete this last decision, then you will reduce the impact of your plans and may cause harm to your heirs. I know it is hard enough to talk about money—even harder talking about money and death. You have to make a conscious decision to do so, and then *just do it.*

Here's the underlying principle of the Talk Decision:

THE EXPECTATION PRINCIPLE ➲ Communicate to align expectations with plans.

WEALTH TRANSFER DECISION-MAKING PROCESS

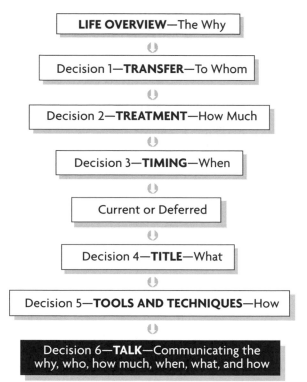

The aim of the Expectation Principle is to get everyone on the same page with no surprises. Try to avoid creating a "coping gap" for your heirs. Bruce Wilkinson, author of *The Prayer of Jabez,* first shared the coping gap concept with me. If the expectations are at one level and reality is at a much different level, then the difference between them is a coping gap.

So, let's say you have an adult child who is expecting about a $500,000 inheritance. You plan on giving substantially to mission work in your state, and your child actually receives only a $5,000 inheritance. That is a $495,000 coping gap! An heir may have difficulty coping with a gift that is significantly different from his or her expectations. Hopefully the heir hasn't spent that money yet.

It can work the other way too. Let's say that your children are expecting, according to their best guess, about $20,000 each. A lawyer contacts them and informs them they will receive $2 million each because of some mutual funds tucked away that grew over the years. Then, the surprise—although a pleasant one—may be difficult for them and their families to deal with.

I have regularly seen this coping gap occur. How can you help your adult children have the right expectations? How can they know your plans? Talk. Communicate. Have a family conference while you are alive. Of all the ideas I have presented in this book, I think you and your heirs may receive the most benefit from this one.

You see, you will have a family conference. It's just a matter of whether you will be alive to attend. Every family has a family conference in the attorney's office after a death occurs to read a will. Wouldn't it be far better to have the family conference prior to your death? Then, you can have an opportunity to teach, share, and explain your reasoning to your heirs. A family conference can be an invaluable time of bringing a family closer together. Parents, children, and grandchildren can understand each other better. For the heirs, it is important to establish proper expectations.

I recently received a request from Dr. Roger Birkman to help him and his wife decide whether to transfer his company. A godly man who desired to be a good steward, Dr. Birkman was being pressured by a charity to turn over his company and products for charitable use. He felt uneasy about this because he had planned to transfer the company he had founded to his daughters. I told them I would meet with them. My only requirement was that every member of the family attend.

All of the family and I later met in Texas. It was not a very large family. The Birkmans had two daughters, one married and one unmarried. Their son-in-law, and a grandchild who recently graduated from college, attended too.

My role was to facilitate their discussions, not to give them an answer. I learned that Dr. Birkman, now age eighty-two, had created a psychological testing system, called the Birkman Method®, with worldwide acceptance and applicability.

For more than forty years, Fortune 500 corporations, government entities, and organizations of every type have used the Birkman tests for individual and organizational development, team building, and management training. More than 1.5 million Americans have benefited from The Birkman Method® with more rewarding careers, marriages, and family life.

Dr. Birkman felt that God gave him the message to create the tests. Fifty years ago, he was working on a project for the U.S. Air Force. He realized that Jesus' Sermon on the Mount says if you see a speck in your brother's eye, then examine the log in your own eye. The light bulb went off. He thought that it might be possible to find out more about people by asking them what they think about other people instead of themselves. He designed a whole psychological testing system around the idea of asking people about other people. A person is essentially how he sees others.

The resulting company has grown with consistent profits as its psychological tests have helped many people and organizations. Dr. Birkman recognized that God owned it all. He has rarely even marketed his product. He considers it a gift from God— the more it's used the better. Unfortunately, others have taken advantage of him over the years, but the product itself and his company is worth many millions of dollars.

As we discussed these matters, all the family members were able to hear the father's powerful testimony, how he considered the company to be an important stewardship responsibility, and how the company had provided for his family and for their generous giving. I could sense the very positive benefits that younger family members were receiving. Also, the parents had an opportunity to hear what their children had a heart for.

We talked about the wealth transfer process and the underlying principles. As we began to address their specific question of transferring ownership of the company now, I asked, "Dr. Birkman, the fundamental question I have is this: Do you trust your daughters?"

The parents thought about it and talked quietly among themselves. Finally, they both said, "Yeah, we really do trust them."

I said, "If you really trust them, then you can trust them with the company, right? You can trust their future stewardship of this vision and ministry that God has given you, right?"

"That's right." The Birkmans nodded.

We then spent several hours discussing various other aspects of their life goals and wealth transfer plans. Toward the end of our time together, I turned and out of the blue (pardon the unintended pun) asked the daughters a question, "Let's say that your dad has been dead for five years. You have been running the company and it has gone very well. A large, publicly owned company approaches you with an offer of $100 million for the company. What are you going to do?"

Without a moment's hesitation, the younger daughter blurted "Sell it!"

A brief, awkward silence followed. I then asked Dr. Birkman, "How do you feel about that?"

He repeated aloud, almost to himself, "Hmmm . . . I said I trusted them, didn't I?"

I said, "That's right."

He thought for a moment longer. "Then it must have been the right decision."

I concluded, "Then you can transfer the company to your daughters." Dr. Birkman could trust the daughters to run it according to his principles. Since the daughters knew his heart and they themselves had giving hearts, Dr. Birkman didn't feel it was necessary to place the ownership of the company in a single ministry's hands. Those who knew him even better would continue his heritage of giving.

If the Birkman family had not held that family conference, the daughters might have been concerned that their father would not want the company sold. They might have struggled, wondering if they did have their father's trust. I have seen many mature, intelligent children paralyzed by indecision concerning assets they have inherited. They say things like "We can never sell the family farm that father built"—even though no one in the family farms or lives near the farm.

HOW A FAMILY CONFERENCE CAN HELP YOUR FAMILY

If you are like most parents, you are not comfortable discussing and developing wealth transfer plans with your children. In my experience, adult children are even less comfortable bringing up such issues. They may wish to help, but don't want to be perceived as nosy or greedy. A family conference can provide tremendous benefits to all the family members as well as peace of mind.

There are many purposes and positive results for family conferences. First and foremost, it is an opportunity for *increased understanding through communication.* As parents, we are responsible for training our children in all areas of life, including the financial area. The family conference offers parents the opportunity to communicate their philosophy, beliefs, and values regarding finances to their children, as well as to communicate financial decisions that will affect the children. Although the parents have a right to do with their assets as they desire, the family conference will allow for dialogue concerning important issues while all parties are present, rather than after a death (when the usual "family conference" occurs).

Because of this healthy communication, the family conference will enhance family harmony. The family conference gives your heirs a chance to hear from you—your heart, your wishes. It also gives them the permission and opportunity to ask questions.

Communicating about money promotes harmony and often avoids the bitterness that may be generated over money decisions.

A second purpose for the family conference is to *pass on wisdom*. It is an opportunity for Mom and Dad to begin to teach their adult children (and perhaps grandchildren) about investment planning, charitable giving, estate planning, and other financial responsibilities. Children can see their parents implementing and modeling wise financial stewardship. Seeing their parents plan, the children will be more likely to plan.

Another purpose is to *specifically discuss the wealth transfer process* for that family. Mom and Dad can explain to their children their current estate plan and why they have set it up that way. Together the family can discuss amounts to be given to charity and even select the specific charities. Reasons for equal and unequal distribution to the children can be explained. The children can be honest about their feelings regarding the amounts their parents are leaving to them.

As we have already discussed, many Christians may improperly believe that just because they have four children, their estate should be split equally among them. Yet the scriptural precedent is that the money should be left to those who have demonstrated sound stewardship. If we leave money to someone with whom we have not left wisdom, it can be a devastating situation. Therefore, in many cases discussing wealth transfer can be a catalyst to help children get "on board" financially and become fiscally responsible.

Yet another purpose for family conferences is to *discuss lifetime (current) giving*. Parents should be careful not to deprive their children while enriching charities. I realize I've written several pages urging you to consider gifts to charity instead of children, but remember we're talking about balance and doing what God wants done with His funds. Does he really want you to completely cut off your kids and give everything to charity? Many children could become bitter when they see their parents withhold from them to give to others. Do you recall the family I mentioned in chapter 4 who realized that such a decision might push their son away from Christ? As I've stressed, these decisions are yours to make because God has made you the steward of these assets. But communicating with your family members will help them understand the motivation behind your decisions and might help avoid much bitterness.

The most effective family conferences involve a facilitator (such as a trusted financial adviser or attorney) who directs and mediates the discussion. Mom, Dad, the children, and their spouses (if appropriate) are present. Other advisers (an insurance agent or accountant, for example) may also be present if decisions involving them will take place. However, a family conference may simply involve the parents sitting down with their children and explaining what they are doing financially and why. The timing of the conference depends on the specific goal to be discussed. You could start as early as when your kids reach their teens or wait until they are older and more mature before involving them in your wealth transfer plans. Remember that you are not asking their permission—you are the steward with the decision-making authority—but you are involving them.

TALK, SHARE, DISCLOSE, AND THEN TALK SOME MORE

Many people avoid making the difficult decision of wealth transfer because they want to avoid conflict. The parents, as they age, mainly desire family harmony. They don't want their kids to argue. They don't want their kids to be upset that money is going to charity. Unfortunately, an "avoidance" approach fosters conflict and possible hard feelings. By not talking about these issues, parents (and adult children) generate more uncertainty, more anxiety, a greater potential for the coping gap, and escalated conflict after the parents' death.

When it comes to inherited wealth, the person who inherits it often feels the obligation to the parent or to the grandparent. Consequently, the heir doesn't do anything with it. As I've mentioned earlier, sometimes mature, responsible adults become paralyzed when managing inherited assets. I have seen this regularly with inherited stock in my experience with financial planning. The inheritors say irrational things based on sentimental feelings like, "We can never sell that stock. Grandpa gave that to us from his estate. He always held it. So should we." Or, "Dad thought this was a good stock, so I am not going to sell it."

Family conferences give the recipients the freedom to exercise stewardship over the wealth the way they feel led. That is the reason you have that conversation. Is it easy? No. Do you have just one conversation for all of time? Probably not. Several discussions may be needed. But God didn't allow you to accumulate this wealth by doing the easy thing or taking shortcuts. You can't expect to transfer wealth successfully to the next steward that way either!

All your stuff will pass to someone else. Whoever gets it will be significantly affected by it. And that someone needs to know your thoughts, plans, and desires. There is a lot at stake here for your heirs, and you have an obligation, yes *obligation,* to prepare them for what's coming.

As I was researching materials for this book, I came across an old article in my files from *Forbes* magazine about how the well-known Kennedy family fared with its wealth. The patriarch, Joseph Kennedy, was an adept businessman. Although some may argue how ethical certain practices were, Joe Kennedy was successful in controlling a chain of movie houses, a movie studio, prime real estate in various cities, and liquor distribution companies.

However, none of his nine children and almost none of his twenty-nine grandchildren has shown any interest or skill in business or managing money. The Kennedy clan is very adept at spending the money. Although they remain far from the poor house, some have estimated their dwindling fortune may not last past the next generation.

The *Forbes* article identified a possible culprit for the lack of business acumen in the descendents:

> Blame Joseph P. himself, the founding father of the fortune. Many families don't believe in talking about business at the dinner table. Joseph Kennedy took that one step further. He didn't believe in talking business to his family at all. "We never discussed money in the house because, well, money isn't important," old Joe told one of his son Jack's biographers.[1]

A somewhat surprising attitude from someone who devoted his life to earning money. Some people think they earn too much to talk to their families, while others think they earn too little to talk to their families. I don't think you can err on the side of talking too much. Even the smallest property items—that vase, china set, box of tools, or chair—can cause sparks to fly among the heirs after death. Even these minor asset bequests merit family discussion.

The families who have a family conference, meeting, or retreat to discuss their wealth transfer plans rarely regret it. Communication is the final and very important step for implementing your wealth transfer plans.

WHAT IF...

Your grandfather, usually very private about money matters, sat down with you before he died and explained his hopes for how you would use the inheritance he planned on leaving you specifically for paying off student loans, funding mission trips, and paying for an annual vacation for your family. How would the discussion have affected your use of the inheritance? Your memory of your grandfather? Your feelings of closeness to your grandfather for the remainder of his life?

MAY I ASK A FOLLOW-UP QUESTION?

Q. *We are ready to have a family discussion with our four adult children, three of whom are financially responsible and one who isn't. We would like to give them equal amounts of money and stock, about $30,000 each, after giving a certain designated amount to our favorite ministries. However, because of the one's irresponsibility, we do not feel comfortable giving her the full amount at this time.*

In our family conference, is it appropriate to explain to her our desire to leave her the same but our hesitation in doing so? Should we make the gift conditional on her improving her money management skills, or do we just hope she'll get the implication? We're afraid that discussing this in front of the other children may cause her to feel embarrassed and drive her away. Should we speak with her alone first and give her a time limit and goals for improvement?

A. Keep focused on your purpose of restoration. With this in mind, then you have to ask the question: Will a family conference accomplish this purpose? Is this going to be better for her or worse for her?

I would recommend that you not embarrass her. Because you want to draw her closer and influence change, it would seem that speaking privately would be the best. I wouldn't think you are obligated to share with the other children how you are treating her. Share with her your deeply held stewardship beliefs. Ask her what her goals are. Perhaps you can help her set those goals together and you can provide encouraging accountability.

Other creative techniques to consider may include paying for a session with a financial planner. Or, give her three dollars for each dollar of debt she repays or every dollar she saves—using the $30,000 you were planning to give. Be sure to walk the fine line between positive motivation and inappropriate control.

JUST DO IT RIGHT!

PASSING ON A
TARGETED LEGACY OF GIVING

When asked by adults what he wanted to be when he grew up, George Dayton replied, "A minister." However, when the depression of 1873 began, George embarked on a business career. After stints in banking and real estate, he founded the Dayton's department store in Minneapolis, the beginning of a very successful retail empire.[2]

Even before possessing great wealth, George was committed to giving to God. He strongly believed in tithing, even when he was only earning several hundred dollars a year or during bad times, because "tithing is putting evangelism into action."[3] He also believed that tithing was the starting point for giving; his meticulous records show he was giving away 40 percent of his income at age thirty.

In 1911, George sold a third of the store to each son. He provided oversight and assistance but allowed the sons to manage the store. In 1921, George received an appreciation letter from a minister that Dayton had supported since seminary. The letter stated that "most men spend all their time making money. You evidently spend not a little time in thinking how to give it away."

Concerned about the possible effect of wealth upon his children, George later shared the letter with his adult children and instructed them,

> I can truly say to you, my children, that nothing brings as much pleasure to your father and mother as doing something for others. Our hope is that our children will catch the spirit of it and find great pleasure in their passing on to others some of the good things which God has brought to them.[4]

This "family conference" no doubt helped his sons and then his grandsons carry on the Dayton family tradition of wise business practices and generous giving. As George practiced the Wisdom Principle, so his son Nelson brought his sons (George's grandsons) into the business under his oversight. These grandsons of George Dayton grew the retail business and expanded the Dayton Corporation. The company acquired other stores, including Hudson's, Mervyn's, and Marshall Field and Co. The Dayton grandsons created a discount store concept in 1962, called Target, which became the company's most profitable store. The company renamed itself in 2000 from Dayton's to the Target Corporation.

In 1946, near the beginning of their management of the company, the George Dayton grandsons instituted a policy of giving 5 percent of the company's pretax profits to charity. At the time, 5 percent was the maximum amount deductible for corporations under the tax code; the Dayton Corporation was only the second company to institute such a policy.

Kenneth Dayton, one of the grandsons of George Dayton, became a public advocate for giving. He had started as a tither and carefully tracked his giving for more than fifty years. In what would make Grandpa George Dayton proud, Kenneth Dayton identified nine stages of giving and he encourages others to progress through these stages. He acknowledged he is in the seventh stage and trying for the final stages:

1. *Minimal Response*—Giving because we were asked and only because we were asked.

2. *Involvement and Interest*—As soon as one becomes in-volved . . . giving becomes more meaningful.

3. *As Much as Possible*—Giving this amount requires a plan and a budget.

4. *Maximum Allowable*—Giving the most that IRS allows as deductible.

5. *Beyond the Max*—No longer would we let the IRS tell us how much (or how little) we could give . . . [however], we no longer had a benchmark . . . we, therefore, needed to invent one.

6. *Percentage of Wealth*—Until we started to measure our giving against our wealth, we did not fully realize how much we could give away and still live very comfortably.

7. *Capping Wealth*—Giving each year a percent of one's wealth forces one to start thinking about the relative im-portance of increasing giving vs. increasing wealth.

8. *Reducing the Cap*—We can visualize the possibility of do-ing so . . . we cannot say whether we will ever have the courage.

9. *Bequests*—Having given our heirs enough assets, we are able to leave almost all our remaining assets [to charities].[5]

"... AND ON WALL STREET TODAY TRADING WAS SUSPENDED IN RESPONSE TO RENEWED RUMORS THAT MONEY ISN'T EVERYTHING!"

CONCLUSION

At the memorial service for Bill Bright, founder of Campus Crusade for Christ, Pastor Howard Edington, Senior Minister of First Presbyterian Church, Orlando, Florida, gave a powerful message about the following passage:

> *Now a man came up to Jesus and asked, "Teacher, what good thing must I do to get eternal life?"*
>
> *"Why do you ask me about what is good?" Jesus replied. "There is only One who is good. If you want to enter life, obey the commandments."*
>
> *"Which ones?" the man inquired.*
>
> *Jesus replied, "'Do not murder, do not commit adultery, do not steal, do not give false testimony, honor your father and mother,' and 'love your neighbor as yourself.'"*
>
> *"All these I have kept," the young man said. "What do I still lack?"*
>
> *Jesus answered, "If you want to be perfect, go, sell your possessions*

and give to the poor, and you will have treasure in heaven. Then come, follow me."

When the young man heard this, he went away sad, because he had great wealth.

Then Jesus said to his disciples, "I tell you the truth, it is hard for a rich man to enter the kingdom of heaven." (Matthew 19:16–23)

In looking at this encounter, Pastor Edington noted that the young man had so much going for him. He . . .

- ➲Was the right age (young)
- ➲Asked the right questions
- ➲Asked the right Person (Jesus)
- ➲Received the right answers
- ➲But made the wrong choice

Pastor Edington continued, "I've always wondered what would have happened if he had made the right choice?" In a great tribute to Bill Bright, who gave up a successful business career to start Campus Crusade for Christ, he said, "Now I know what would have happened. The world is changed."

My hope for you is that you will have made the right choice in your wealth transfer plans.

As Plato wisely observed, "The beginning is the most important part of any work." Begin with the hardest and most important part of the wealth transfer decisions—thinking through the transfer and treatment decisions. When you know to whom your wealth will go and how much, then you can better determine the proper timing and titling. After these decisions, then the tools and techniques become more obvious. When your tools and techniques are implemented, you are ready and confident to share your wealth transfer plans with your family and others.

The proper wealth transfer plans are part of a faithful steward's finishing well. May all those who know and follow Jesus Christ hear Him say, "Well done, my good and faithful servant."

> *Then you will win favor and a good name in the sight of God and man. . . . In all your ways acknowledge him, and he will make your paths straight.* (Proverbs 3:4, 6)

APPENDIX
THE BEST INHERITANCE OF ALL

Throughout this book, you have read about planning, inheritance, death, and heirs. Please allow me to tell you how these same topics can have another and more important application than preparing a will and leaving stuff. The most important decision concerning your death is where you will live for eternity.

The Bible provides a fantastic promise that "we might become heirs having the hope of eternal life" (Titus 3:7). This is the best inheritance because it is "an inheritance that can never perish, spoil or fade—kept in heaven for you" (1 Peter 1:4).

How can we receive this inheritance? How can we be certain we are heirs of God? I like how Campus Crusade for Christ explains it in the *Four Spiritual Laws* tract:

WE MUST INDIVIDUALLY RECEIVE JESUS CHRIST AS SAVIOR AND LORD; THEN WE CAN KNOW AND EXPERIENCE GOD'S LOVE AND PLAN FOR OUR LIVES.

WE MUST RECEIVE CHRIST

"Yet to all who received him, to those who believed in his name, he gave the right to become children of God." (John 1:12)

WE RECEIVE CHRIST THROUGH FAITH

"By grace you have been saved, through faith—and this not from yourselves, it is the gift of God—not by works, so that no one can boast." (Ephesians 2:8–9)

WHEN WE RECEIVE CHRIST, WE EXPERIENCE A NEW BIRTH
(Read John 3:1–8.)

WE RECEIVE CHRIST THROUGH PERSONAL INVITATION

[Jesus Christ speaking] *"Here I am! I stand at the door and knock. If anyone hears my voice and opens the door, I will come in and eat with him, and he with me."* (Revelation 3:20)

Receiving Christ involves turning to God from self (repentance) and trusting Christ to come into our lives to forgive our sins and to make us what He wants us to be. Just to agree intellectually that Jesus Christ is the Son of God and that He died on the cross for our sins is not enough. Nor is it enough to have an emotional experience. We receive Jesus Christ by faith, as an act of the will.

YOU CAN RECEIVE CHRIST RIGHT NOW BY FAITH THROUGH PRAYER (PRAYER IS TALKING WITH GOD)

God knows your heart and is not so concerned with your words as He is with the attitude of your heart. The following is a suggested prayer:

> Lord Jesus, I need You. Thank You for dying on the cross for my sins. I open the door of my life and receive You as my Savior and Lord. Thank You for forgiving my sins and giving me eternal life. Take control of the throne of my life. Make me the kind of person You want me to be.

Does this prayer express the desire of your heart? If it does, I invite you to pray this prayer right now, and Christ will come into your life, as He promised.[1]

The greatest wealth transfer that ever occurred was when Jesus died for you. "For this reason Christ is the mediator of a new covenant, that those who are called may receive the promised eternal inheritance—now that he has died as a ransom to set them free from the sins committed" (Hebrews 9:15).

You are now part of His family. He loves you and treats you uniquely as His child. "Now if we are children, then we are heirs—heirs of God and co-heirs with Christ" (Romans 8:17a).

With Christ, you are rich indeed—both in this life and, more importantly, for eternity.

NOTES

CHAPTER 1: CONFESSIONS OF PROCRASTINATION

1. John Havens and Paul Schervish, "Why the $41 Trillion Wealth Transfer Estimate Is Still Valid: A Review of Challenges and Questions," *The Journal of Gift Planning* 7, No. 1 (January 2003): 11–15, 47–50.

CHAPTER 2: THE WEALTH TRANSFER PROCESS AND LIFE OVERVIEW

1. Obtained from the International Programs Center and U.S. Population Division of the U.S. Bureau of the Census.

2. Joseph Frazier Wall, ed. *The Andrew Carnegie Reader* (Pittsburgh: Univ. of Pittsburgh Press, 1992), 41.

3. The Carnegie Corporation of New York Website at www.carnegie.org.

4. Robert T. Grimm Jr., ed. *Notable American Philanthropists* (Westport, Conn.: Greenwood, 2002), 54–55.

5. Andrew Carnegie, "Wealth," *North American Review,* 148, no. 391 (June 1889): 653, 657–62.

CHAPTER 3: YOUR TRANSFER DECISION

1. CNN, 18 September 1997. (www.cnn.com)

2. Antonio Regalado, "Billionaire Opens His Deep Pockets for Climate Theory," *Wall Street Journal,* 17 July 2003.

3. Eric Gibson, "Can $100 Million Help Make Poetry Matter?" *Wall Street Journal,* 26 November 2002.

4. "The New (But Not New) Giving," *Worth* magazine, April 2000, 145.

5. Randy Alcorn, *The Treasure Principle: Discovering the Secret of Joyful Giving* (Sisters, Oreg.: Multnomah, 2001), 17.

6. Ibid., 40, 43.

7. Website of "Financial Planning for Women" (www.andersonplan.com.au. htm).

8. Robert T. Grimm Jr. ed., *Notable American Philanthropists* (Westport, Conn.: Greenwood, 2002), 315.

9. Bertram Wyatt-Brown, *Lewis Tappan and the Evangelical War Against Slavery* (Baton Rouge, La.: Louisiana State Univ., 1997), 70.

10. Grimm, *American Philanthropists,* 317.

11. Wyatt-Brown, *Lewis Tappan and the Evangelical War Against Slavery,* 212.

CHAPTER 4: YOUR TREATMENT DECISION

1. Information obtained from the Chick-fil-A company Website at www.chick-fil-a.com.

2. Information obtained from press releases on the Chick-fil-A company Website at www.chick-fil-a.com.

CHAPTER 5: YOUR TIMING DECISION

1. Ronald W. Blue, *Generous Giving* (Grand Rapids: Zondervan, 1997), 136.

2. Stephen M. Pollan and Mark Levine, *Die Broke* (New York: HarperBusiness, 1997), 15, 17.

3. Robynn Tysver, "Warren Buffet Hits Campaign Trail," *The San Diego Union-Tribune,* Associated Press, 16 October 1994, p. I-1.

4. Dave Ramsey, *More Than Enough* (New York: Penguin, 1999), 281.

5. Claude Rosenberg Jr., *Wealthy and Wise* (Boston, Mass.: Little, Brown, and Company, 1994), 7, 38–39, 165.

6. Oseola McCarty, *Simple Wisdom for Rich Living* (Atlanta: Longstreet Press, 1996), x.

7. Ibid., 17.

8. Robert T. Grimm Jr., ed., *Notable American Philanthropists* (Westport, Conn.: Greenwood, 2002), 205.

9. McCarty, *Simple Wisdom,* 10.

10. Ibid., 36.

11. Ibid., 75.

CHAPTER 6: YOUR TITLE DECISION

1. Randy Alcorn, *The Treasure Principle: Discovering the Secret of Joyful Giving,* (Sisters, Oreg.: Multnomah, 2001), 74.

2. Material summarized from LeTourneau's biographical information included in his autobiography, *Mover of Men and Mountains* (Chicago: Moody, 1967) and a biographical sketch from LeTourneau University's site at www.letu. edu.

CHAPTER 7: YOUR TOOLS AND TECHNIQUES DECISION

1. Jay C. Grelen, "Why Everyone's Looking Up to David Robinson," *Christian Reader,* March/April 1998, vol. 36, no. 2, 20.

2. "David Robinson: Founding a Legacy of Leadership," article at www. philanthropyintexas.com.

3. Grelen, "Why Everyone's Looking Up to David Robinson," 20.

CHAPTER 8: YOUR TALK DECISION

1. Laura Jereski, "Shirtsleeves to Shirtsleeves," *Forbes,* 21 October 1991, 34.

2. Robert T. Grimm Jr. ed. *Notable American Philanthropists* (Westport, Conn.: Greenwood, 2002), 73–76.

3. Bruce B. Dayton, and Ellen B. Green, *George Draper Dayton: A Man of Parts* (Minneapolis: Privately printed, 1997), 416.

4. Ibid., 433.

5. Kenneth N. Dayton, *The Stages of Giving* (Washington, D.C.: Independent Sector, 1999).

APPENDIX: THE BEST INHERITANCE OF ALL

1. "Have You Heard of the Four Spiritual Laws?" © Copyrighted 1965, 1968 by Campus Crusade for Christ, New Life Publications.

RON BLUE has thirty years of experience starting two successful financial services firms that have encouraged thousands in meeting their personal financial objectives. He is currently president of Kingdom Advisors, whose mission is to help Christian financial professionals incorporate biblical wisdom into their advice and counsel, as well as to connect Christians seeking financial counsel with biblically wise Christian financial professionals. Ron is the author of sixteen books, including the bestselling, *The New Master Your Money*. Ron and his wife, Judy, have five children and nine grandchildren, and live in Atlanta.

JEREMY WHITE has been a certified public accountant for more than fifteen years with financial experience in public accounting and industry. His CPA firm specializes in retirement planning, estate planning, and wealth management for those in the second half of life. Jeremy assisted Larry Burkett and Crown Ministries as a writing consultant in updating their *Family Financial Planning Workbook*, and worked with Larry and Ron Blue on *Wealth to Last*. He has been a frequent guest on the *How to Manage Your Money* radio broadcast. Jeremy resides in Paducah, Kentucky with his wife and two daughters.

KINGDOM ⚜ ADVISORS

As President of Kingdom Advisors, Ron has committed
the balance of his professional life to teaching others
what God has given him the privilege of learning over
his thirty year career serving financial professionals
and clients.

Ron is leading an international effort of dedicated,
competent, and spiritually passionate financial advisors
who are serious about making their lives count for
Christ.

As financial professionals, they are men and women
who recognize the unique opportunity they have
to see Kingdom impact through integrating biblical
wisdom in their advice and counsel to their
clients.

For more information about Kingdom Advisors,
visit www.kingdomadvisors.org
or call (404) 497.7680

Ron Blue serves on the Board of Directors of the following
Christian stewardship organizations:

CROWN FINANCIAL MINISTRIES
Teaching People God's Financial Principles

Crown Financial Ministries, founded by Larry Burkett (1939-2003) and Howard Dayton, is the world's largest Christian financial ministry, providing the following to teach people God's financial principles:

- Over 200 instructive materials for small groups, children, single parents, and the International community.

- A church Bible study program.
- Four national and two international radio programs.
- A comprehensive Web site.
- An award-winning full-color newsletter.
- Personality and career products.

For more information on the ministry of *Crown*, visit us online at
www.crown.org or call **1-800-722-1976**

Generous Giving is a privately funded nonprofit ministry that seeks to encourage givers of all income levels—as well as ministry leaders, pastors and teachers and professional advisors—to experience the joy of giving and embrace a lifestyle of generosity, according to God's word and Christ's example.

Launched in 2000 by the Maclellan Foundation, *Generous Giving* offers an array of practical tools that encourage generosity, including the *Generous Giving Marketplace*, an online classified listing of hundreds of global funding opportunities posted by Christian ministries.

Learn more about *Generous Giving* by visiting **www.GenerousGiving.org**

THE NATIONAL CHRISTIAN FOUNDATION

The National Christian Foundation embodies the concept of smart Christian giving. Founded 22 years ago by Terry Parker, Larry Burkett and Ron Blue, *NCF* has helped people put hundreds of millions of dollars into Christian ministries and charities.

Our Stewardship Funds provide an immediate tax deduction and allow for gifts to grow until the donor determines which organizations to support. *NCF's* ability to accept gifts of real estate and other non-liquid assets allows the donor to advance their charitable goals and maximize tax benefits.

To learn more about the ministry of *NCF*, visit
www.nationalchristian.com or call **1-800-681-6223**